Careers in Real Estate

2006 Edition

WetFeet Insider Guide

Helping you make smarter career decisions.

WetFeet, Inc.

The Folger Building
101 Howard Street
Suite 300
San Francisco, CA 94105

Phone: (415) 284-7900 or 1-800-926-4JOB
Fax: (415) 284-7910
Website: www.WetFeet.com

Careers in Real Estate

2006 Edition
ISBN: 1-58207-510-7

Table of Contents

Real Estate at a Glance

Opportunity Overview

- As a whole, the real estate industry has performed better over the past few years than almost every sector of the U.S. economy, and sluggish sectors, such as commercial office space and apartment rentals, seem to be picking up, though rising interest rates should eventually put a damper on homebuilding.

- The real estate industry is enormous, employing around 5 million people. However, opportunities within the industry vary greatly, even within a single job title.

- Companies tend to be parochial and local in scope due to the subtleties of different geographic markets. Even companies with national and international operations function more as federations of small companies than as centralized powers.

- Opportunities for undergraduates, MBAs, and midcareer professionals are out there, but be prepared to network as industry professionals tend to hire from personal contacts and relationships rather than through formal recruiting practices.

- For those interested in real estate development and acquisition, opportunities to get a foot in the door as financial analysts are available at insurance companies, pension funds, and other financial services firms.

- The industry thrives on performance-based compensation and offers few perks and benefits. People who succeed in real estate tend to be entrepreneurial.

- In real estate, what goes up must come down. It is not a wise career choice for the faint of heart. Successful real estate practitioners are those who can endure the industry's downturns.

- Those who are truly successful in the industry have the opportunity to change the face of communities and cities.

Major Pluses of the Real Estate Industry

• You have the opportunity to make staggering amounts of money.

• You get to build many lasting client relationships and can mix business with pleasure.

• You have a great deal of flexibility in scheduling your time.

• You can flex your entrepreneurial muscles.

• You get to work on and execute exciting deals.

Major Minuses of the Real Estate Industry

• The hours can be long, especially when you're establishing your place in the industry. Work can creep into personal time by way of cell phone calls from clients at any time of the day, any day of the week.

• The pay can be low starting out, especially in brokerage companies.

• The industry can be highly competitive.

• Most positions offer few perks and benefits, especially for brokers and agents.

• The real estate industry is highly location-specific. Knowledge in one market often doesn't carry over to another region. You can, therefore, be tethered to the geography in which you start your career.

• There is no set career path; you have to carve out your own niche in the industry.

Recruiting Overview

The top three methods for establishing a career in real estate are networking, networking, and more networking.

Some larger companies and financial services firms actively recruit for financial analyst and support positions. Insurance companies and pension funds are known to have substantial real estate investments. Large investment bankers like Merrill Lynch and Goldman Sachs have private placement real estate groups with positions for analysts (undergraduates) and associates (MBAs). Your best chance of getting into real estate investment without a real estate background is to work in one of these firms.

Otherwise, without a personal connection, breaking into the industry can be difficult. Positions that serve as the best platforms for advancement in the industry—commercial broker or development project manager—are usually attained through connections with people already in the industry. "Most people get into the industry the old-fashioned way," says one insider, "through relationships."

The Industry

Overview

As you drive your Range Rover up the New Jersey Turnpike through *Sopranos* country, you glance up beyond hundreds of acres of landfill and see the lone pencil of the Empire State Building glinting in the distance. You think to yourself, "This is the perfect place for a golf course and housing development—a refuge for hundreds of golf-starved New Yorkers, with homes on the links minutes from Manhattan. And to round it out perhaps some light industrial space. . . ." Your mind races with plans for how to put it all together—government permits, environmental impact reports, financing, a top-tier architect, master contractor, sales agents, and brokers. You get home and tell your girlfriend, swearing her to secrecy. Bad news, she tells you, your project is already underway. Undaunted, you start thinking about the next opportunity.

Thinking big is part and parcel of the real estate industry, and grandiose speculation has created some of America's greatest fortunes. John Jacob Astor traded in his empire of beaver pelts for a gamble on uptown Manhattan real estate and in the process became the richest man in America. Arthur Levitt's own development virtually created that fixture of American life: the suburbs. More recently, moguls like Sam "the grave dancer" Zell and the perennially overreaching Donald Trump have made fantastic fortunes on real estate gambles. Even for nonbillionaires in the industry, the thrill of deal making, the promise of financial reward, the potential to have a lasting impact on cities and communities, and the sociability make real estate a rewarding profession.

The real estate market has undergone dramatic changes in recent years. Real estate investment trusts (REITs) have become major sources of financing for property acquisition and development. According to the National Association of Real Estate Investment Trusts, the total market capitalization of public REITs has grown from about $13 billion in 1991 to more than $300 billion in 190 funds in 2004, causing a revolution in real estate financing, similar to the rise of the individual investor in the stock market.

Sources of financing have been steadily moving from cabals of private investors to public equity, in the form of REITs. With this shift has come more transparency in the market and a slow whittling away of the old boys network for which real estate investment is infamous. This transparency also shines a critical light on investment strategies, which are now subject to public scrutiny, and are therefore more accountable to the will of investors. Families with their savings invested in REITs are unlikely to tolerate the wild swings of fortune of stereotypical real estate tycoons; Wall Street and REITs have had a stabilizing effect on the industry. Finally, mergers and acquisitions have increased the size and scope of firms involved in real estate, with companies like brokerage and hotel franchiser Cendant leading the charge.

Nevertheless, the industry itself is slow to change. Two of the largest real estate investment companies, Donald Trump's Trump Organization and the LeFrak family's Lefrak Organization, are decidedly private and operate almost exclusively in the New York area. With its unpredictable cycles and idiosyncratic geographic markets, the real estate industry continues to defy taming by modern organizational structure.

If you have the right skills and are undaunted by the vicissitudes of the industry, real estate can afford a phenomenally challenging and rewarding career. People skills are paramount in real estate. Everyone, from brokers to investment fund partners, relies on the relationships they forge throughout their careers to find clients and understand the subtleties and caprices of the market. Professional real estate investors need a well-honed financial and analytical tool kit to evaluate the investment potential of properties as well as keen sales and marketing instincts to sell not only their developments, but also their funds to investors. Project management skills are as critical to the tasks of ongoing asset and property management as they are to coordinating large-scale deals. Finally, people who endure in the industry have the fortitude to see themselves through the famine of down markets.

CAREER TRACKS

Job opportunities in the industry are divided into four distinct fields: sales, management, development, and acquisition and analysis. Although crossover among these sectors is possible, most people start out specializing in a specific area.

Sales and Leasing

Sales and leasing includes everything from residential real estate brokers such as Century 21 and Coldwell Banker to larger corporations that broker bigger commercial properties such as office towers. Grubb & Ellis has one of the largest global brokerage divisions, offering sales and leasing services in many U.S. markets and in Europe. Cushman & Wakefield is another giant, with offices nationwide. Its clients are primarily corporations and other institutions, for which it negotiates sales and leases. Trammell Crow Company is a third large player in this sector.

Management

Property managers are responsible for maintaining property values. They deal with tenants, manage finances, and physically tend to the property. Of all the segments of the industry, this one has been hit hardest by the wave of mergers and acquisitions sweeping the industry. For job seekers, this means fewer jobs as companies look to become more efficient and cut redundant staff. However, rising property values has led many "mom and pop" owners to turn over property management to property managers, helping grow revenues and opportunities at many firms.

Development

Developers are responsible for taking a property idea and making it a reality. This is a complex process involving architects, engineers, zoning officials, builders, lenders, and prospective tenants. Development is not always the gravy train some make it out to be. In the early 1990s, when real estate prices crashed, construction dried up and a lot of commercial office space was left vacant. Deprived of rents, a lot of developers had to scramble for survival. Many ventured into other areas of real estate. Today, many of the largest real estate developers are also property owners and managers.

Acquisition and Analysis

Any kind of investing in real estate requires a thorough understanding of how to analyze the value of a property and navigate the maze of land-use regulations, zoning laws, environmental impact reports, financing realities, and other barriers to buying and developing a property. The people who develop, market, and manage REITs and other real estate investments are financial types, often MBAs, who are charged with evaluating and arranging for the purchase of properties.

The Bottom Line

Without solid connections in the industry, you may have a hard time establishing yourself. Real estate veterans rely on the advice of contacts to help make recruiting decisions. Rather than using traditional recruiting processes, firms often bring on new talent through personal networks and word of mouth. It's even harder to break into the elite club of real estate investment finance. Because real estate investment funds often invest in and manage operations of their investments, "they look for candidates with solid operational and finance experience in the industry in addition to a thick Rolodex," according to an insider.

Landing a job at a large financial services firm such as Goldman Sachs, BlackRock, or The Blackstone Group that has a significant real estate investment practice not only adds a lot of cachet to your resume and develops critical finance skills, it also allows you to network with people at real estate advisory firms and developers, precisely the people you need to be in contact with to get ahead in the industry. In addition to candidates with MBAs and heavy hanging financial tool belts, fund managers also look highly on experience in operational roles in large residential and commercial development projects as well as experience in commercial brokerage. While operational roles in development often require construction management backgrounds, commercial brokerage positions have a number of feeder tracks. In addition to candidates with substantial sales experience in other industries, commercial brokerage firms sometimes take in college interns and often promote marketing staffers and similar personnel to broker roles. Note that while there is a path from commercial brokerage to asset management and development, retail brokerage careers offer far less leeway in terms of industry mobility. Put bluntly, if you start in retail brokerage, you'll end in retail brokerage.

If you don't aspire to join the elite ranks of real estate investment management, you still have before you a wealth of rewarding positions in property management, real estate services, and residential brokerages, as well as very challenging development roles in corporate real estate. Beware though: Skills in one real estate market aren't necessarily transferable to other markets. Select your location carefully. And once you're in, be prepared to ride the roller coaster of a cyclical industry. Although the real estate industry is in a protracted boom period right now, veterans assure us that busts will come, and those busts won't be pretty.

Industry Breakdown

Everything we do, commercial and personal, real and virtual, requires space and therefore the land on which space sits. The real estate industry has taken this law of nature and run with it. The real estate industry is powered by agents who work in concert to make land available—physically, legally, and financially—for every imaginable human need. Developers and asset managers invest in and improve land to create a supply of real estate that they anticipate will meet the needs of a population's industrial, commercial, and residential endeavors. Property managers maintain investment property for owners to maximize a property's cash flow and resale value. Brokerage firms match the supply of property that landowners possess with the demand of businesses and individuals. Financial services firms provide the means for developers to improve space and for businesses and individuals to buy or lease space. Finally, a wide variety of ancillary service firms provide a framework to smooth the transaction process and build trust into the system.

In general, the real estate industry is highly fragmented. The largest companies in the industry garner only single-digit market share within their subsectors. Centex, one of the nation's largest homebuilders, controls less than 2 percent of the U.S. new housing market. Sam Zell's Equity Office Properties, the largest real estate investment trust (REIT) in the country, controls only 2 percent of the country's office space. Even as the largest players in every segment of the industry grow and gobble up second-tier firms, they still have yet to achieve anything like true market consolidation. Because the market is so vast and because market knowledge doesn't transfer across regions, most companies tend to focus on segments of individual geographic markets. Homebuilders often focus on regions, such as the Southeast or Southwest—especially in the Sunbelt states where populations are growing, land is plentiful, and the building season is long. An REIT may be active in a particular market—retail, mall retail, office, warehouse, or investment residential—within a region. Smaller firms often operate within a single metropolitan area.

Because of this phenomenon, industry insiders usually spend much of their careers in the same geographic market. Though relocating doesn't necessarily mean starting from scratch, it does mean losing some of your accumulated social and intellectual capital of long-cultivated relationships and hard-won local knowledge.

Within the industry, a large chasm divides the commercial and residential sectors. Firms involved in commercial real estate generally do not participate in the residential market and vice versa. This makes it difficult to leverage skills and experience when switching between sectors.

ASSET ACQUISITION, MANAGEMENT, AND DEVELOPMENT

Asset acquisition, management, and development firms are concerned with real estate as an investment vehicle for their private or public investors. They create the supply in the real estate market. Firms will take green field property or existing developments and improve, manage, and dispose of them in accordance with their investment strategies. Representative types of asset management and development entities include REITs, private investment organizations and funds, advisory companies, commercial developers, and residential developers. The entities differ from one another in characteristics such as investment goals, scope of operation, and legal status.

Real Estate Investment Trusts

REITs, the best known of real estate investment vehicles, are corporations or trusts that use pooled capital to purchase or manage income property. REITs derive their popularity from three factors:

1. They provide liquidity to an otherwise illiquid asset.

2. They allow small investors to participate in real estate investment.

3. They are not subject to federal income tax.

Investment in REITs burgeoned through the 1990s after legislation allowed them to actively manage properties. To qualify as an REIT, an investment trust must

- Pass 90 percent of its income back to shareholders.

- Have at least 100 shareholders with no more than 50 percent of shares owned by five or less shareholders.

- Derive 75 percent of income from real estate.

- Invest 75 percent of assets in real estate.

- Be governed by a board of directors.

- Hold no more than 20 percent taxable subsidiaries.

REITs are divided into three categories based on the types of assets they hold: (1) Equity REITs directly acquire and manage property; (2) mortgage REITs extend credit to property owners and managers; and (3) hybrid REITs perform both functions. Equity REITs are by far the largest of the three types, making up approximately 96 percent of all REITs. Equity REITS are typically further broken down based on the type of properties they hold. Major categories of equity REITs include residential, office, industrial, land, health care, hotel and motel, leisure and entertainment, and retail segments. But REITs often specialize in much more specific types of property assets. For instance, Corrections Corporation of America and Correctional Properties Trust specialize in the management of prison assets.

REITs have become quite popular in recent years. When the economy flatlined at the beginning of the decade and investors scrambled to find alternative investments, they looked to real estate, which offered high yields relative to their risk exposure. This winning combination attracted a surge of investment dollars, and REITs have given investors happy returns.

Primary career opportunities in REITs include asset manager, analyst, landlord, sales, broker, and property manager roles as well as finance, marketing, and support roles.

Larger REITs do some major recruiting, but this is mostly for property manager and leasing agent type roles.

Private Investment Organizations

Private investment organizations are in many ways the venture capitalists in the real estate world. Like REITs, they pool investor capital into investment properties. However, unlike REITs, they solicit capital from a small number of private investors or institutions. Because they aren't beholden to rules governing REITs, they have more leeway in how they invest their funds. Though private investment organizations rank among the largest real estate companies in the United States, like the The Trump Organization, The Irvine Company, and The Lefrak Organization, scores of smaller partnerships and private funds develop and manage real estate assets throughout the country.

Larger investment organizations offer many of the same roles found in REITs. For instance, if an investment firm has a critical mass of space in a market, it will often handle the property management and leasing. Smaller funds, however, will often outsource property management and brokerage roles and focus on competency as asset managers. As with REITs, most of the opportunities within these organizations are in operational roles, with fewer openings for finance roles.

Commercial Developers

Commercial developers act as the hub in the real estate development process. They perform or coordinate land acquisition and assembly, negotiation, government relationships, finance, design, and construction of buildings as well as leasing and sales for commercial, industrial, or residential properties. Because of the cost, scope, and time involved in commercial developments, a single firm rarely performs all functions; instead, developers rely on relationships with firms in allied industries.

For example, in 2004 the golf course development firm EnCap Golf broke ground on a high-profile $1 billion project to develop a golf course, housing, and office complex on four former landfills in the New Jersey Meadowlands across the Hudson River from Manhattan. The firm established broad-reaching partnerships and assembled an extensive team to execute the project. The firm sought to use its own affiliated construction management company, but brought in external financial backing from Cherokee Partners, a real estate venture capital fund. It outsourced design to a team that included the prestigious architecture firm Robert A.M. Stern, as well as golf course, landscape, and environmental architects.

Residential Developers

Residential real estate developers enjoy the distinction of building the ever-expanding American suburbs. Residential real estate development was pioneered by William Levitt, who brought the standardized building techniques he learned during World War II to postwar America. His endless tract of Cape Cod look-alikes, appropriately named Levittown, has been deemed America's first suburb.

Residential developers perform many of the same tasks as their commercial counterparts, but their work is more limited in scope by their end products, which tend to be single-family homes and low-density housing. Like commercial developers, residential developers are involved in coordinating financing, architectural services, and construction management. In an effort to pull in a larger share of the homebuyer's wallet, companies have been moving downstream, offering a whole suite of products including mortgage origination, title services, broadband and phone services, as well as premium options such as kitchen islands and high-end appliances.

The largest homebuilders—Centex, Pulte, Lennar, and KB Home—are organized as public corporations. Of the public companies, many like Lennar have family members that own majority or controlling shares of the company. While the industry is by no means an oligopoly, the leading companies have consolidated the industry in recent years through a rash of acquisitions. Meanwhile, low interest rates and rapidly rising home prices have buoyed the industry's growth, with many builders posting record numbers of homes built in 2004. Forecasts for 2005, despite rising interest rates, remain strong. In February 2005, housing starts rose a half percent over those in January, and 15.8 percent over year-earlier results—a 21-year high that surprised many analysts. While prices are expected to rise more modestly in 2005 than in 2004, and sales fall from nearly 1.2 million to somewhere between 1.06 and 1.13 million, the sector remains strong.

BROKERAGE

Real estate brokerages match supply with demand; they bring together parties interested in selling, buying, leasing, or exchanging property. Real estate agents, who directly sell properties, must work under a broker and typically turn over a portion of their commission to the brokerage, or they can obtain the extra licensing necessary to become brokers themselves. Typically, brokers represent owners, buyers, or lessees, though firms rarely represent both buyer/tenant and seller/landlord in the same transaction. While residential brokers will represent both buying and selling parties, commercial brokers specialize in representing tenants, sellers, or buildings. Brokers split a fee ranging from 6 to 8 percent of the transaction. In both commercial and residential real estate, individual states require agents and brokers to obtain licenses to represent clients. Requirements for gaining credentials vary from state to state; however, the broker's license requires more education and work experience. Almost every state requires that agents practice under a broker.

Though most brokers and agents work for larger firms and thus benefit from their employer's support services and branding, they view themselves as independent businesses. Many brokerage companies offer only minimal benefits and put brokers on 100 percent commission-based compensation. The amount brokers earn depends on the market in which they operate. Brokers in markets with high real estate prices such as Manhattan and San Francisco tend to do much better than those in less-affected markets.

Commercial Brokerage

The largest brokerage firms such as CBRE, ONCOR International, Colliers International, Cushman & Wakefield, and New American International are national or global in scope. While smaller firms might specialize in one of the subsectors of commercial real estate, the larger firms will run multiple practices around office, industrial, retail, and multifamily residential segments. These firms augment brokerage functions with suites of other real estate services such as property management, facilities management, appraisal, and financial and consulting services.

Commercial brokers typically represent tenants, sellers, or buildings. Client brokers are least likely of the three groups to receive a base salary, but have the most upside potential. Seller brokers have a similar pay structure, whereas building brokers are more likely to have a stable, but lower income. Sales cycles are long in commercial real estate; a broker may work with a client for years before executing a transaction. "My last deal took 2½ years before we signed," says one insider. Moreover, commercial brokerage, as you might expect, is closely tied to the general business cycle. The carnage of the first part of the millennium left a mark on commercial real estate. Office building vacancy rates fell from 18.2 percent in 2003 to 17.4 percent in 2004. Lower rates mean fewer deals and at lower prices—never a good thing if those are the two primary drivers of your salary.

Residential Brokerage

The scope of residential brokerage is more limited than that of commercial brokerage; residential brokerages engage in the sale of single-tenant residential real estate. Residential brokerage firms work under two basic models: the supported services franchise and the independent owner. Under the supported services model, company- or franchisee-owned real estate agencies such as Cendant's Century 21 and Coldwell Banker will offer their brand and support services such as signage, legal teams, and financial analysts to their member agents and brokers in exchange for a sizable portion of commissions. Under the independent owner model, such as that used by RE/MAX, brokers and agents are allowed to use the firm's brand, but receive only minimal support services in exchange for minimal franchise fees.

The role of broker is where most of the opportunities in residential real estate reside, with the best opportunities in growing and high-priced markets. While some see the role as a "housewife's hobby," the potential financial rewards are great. Says one insider, "Stars can make well over a quarter million dollars a year." However, beware if you plan to use your broker experience as a stepping-stone into commercial real estate or development. "You're no better off than coming in as a farmer," says one insider. But in the current market, being in residential brokerage isn't such a bad thing. Unlike the comatose commercial sector, the residential sector is booming; record home sales and continuing high prices are putting not only bread, but also some filet mignon, on the retail broker's table.

PROPERTY MANAGEMENT

Firms in the property management sector generally operate properties for investors and asset management firms. The scope of property management is expansive and ranges from core property management to facilities, construction, and energy management. Property management includes lease administration, building maintenance, tenant management, capital improvements planning, contract administration, financial modeling, and reporting. Construction management includes facility management, landscaping, custodial services, waste management, and security. Energy management covers energy procurement and negotiation, and energy consulting.

Many property management firms bundle their services with commercial real estate brokerage services, or vice versa. Leaders in the property management field include Jones Lang LaSalle, Trammell Crow, Colliers International, and Cushman & Wakefield.

Opportunities for property management roles abound not only in property management firms, but also brokerages, asset management companies, and REITs. Though property management isn't the most direct path to coveted REIT or asset management positions, it does give job seekers exposure to a broad spectrum of positions and professionals throughout the industry.

FINANCING

Financing is the backbone behind the real estate business. Whether it's for a first-time homebuyer or an entrepreneur making the deal of a lifetime, financing will make a real estate dream become a reality. Finance companies run a full spectrum of colors. In the consumer market, financers include quasi-governmental agencies such as Fannie Mae and the Veterans Administration as well as traditional mortgage banks and thrifts. Helping grease the wheels of this sector are a wide range of organizations that help protect individual homebuyers as well as provide them affordable financing. These include mortgage brokers that seek out the best loans for individuals, mortgage insurers that allow low-income families to extend their financial leverage, and loan aggregators such as Freddie Mac, that keep a steady flow of funds available to homebuyers. In the commercial sector, finance options become much more exotic birds. The most popular of these in the public imagination are REITs, those mutual fund–like vehicles that allow small individual investors a stake in large-scale commercial developments. Add to this pension funds and life insurance companies, which look for high, low-risk returns that only real estate can give. Finally, there are a host of private equity funds that assemble capital from both very wealthy individuals and institutional investors and invest in any number of real estate and mortgage vehicles.

Insurance Companies, Pension Funds, and Other Institutional Investors

Life insurance companies and pension funds also invest in real estate in the United States. These risk-averse companies put a significant portion of their portfolios in real estate—which offers highly attractive risk-adjusted returns. Pension funds and life insurance companies each hold approximately 7 percent of the nation's mortgages.

MetLife has more than $36 billion invested in real estate equities, commercial mortgages, and secured investments. Pacific Life Insurance has built a significant practice around mortgages, asset management, and commercial real estate. The nation's largest pension fund, the California Public Employees' Retirement System (CalPERS), has $11.7 billion, or 6.4 percent of its portfolio, invested in real estate, with an 8 percent target. Not all firms have the expertise to manage these properties and will often outsource to boutique asset management companies. Companies like Prudential Financial Services have evolved real estate development groups, offering exposure to the real estate world from within the well-charted waters of corporate America.

Mortgage Financing

Simply put, mortgages are loans used for real estate that have set payback periods and liens against property. The primary financing mechanism for consumers, mortgages are used in both commercial and residential real estate. The process of mortgage financing usually involves mortgage brokers, mortgage bankers, and secondary mortgage institutions.

Mortgage Brokers

Like real estate brokers, mortgage brokers bring together buyers and sellers. Mortgage brokers check if the buyer can qualify for a conforming loan, one that conforms to the qualifications set up by organizations such as Fannie Mae or the Veterans Administration. For buyers that don't qualify, the broker finds the most advantageous traditional loan and negotiates favorable terms with the mortgage bankers.

Mortgage Bankers

Mortgage bankers originate or issue loans to homebuyers. If a loan conforms to terms set by Fannie Mae, Freddie Mac, or another organization, the banker will sell the loan for a fee to that organization. Primary market lenders include mortgage companies, savings and loans, commercial banks, credit unions, and state and local housing finance agencies.

Secondary Mortgage Companies

Secondary mortgage companies purchase mortgages from mortgage originators. Of these companies, the Federal National Mortgage Association, or Fannie Mae, is perhaps the best known. Fannie Mae was founded in 1938 during the Great Depression to prevent a capital crisis in the residential housing market. Fannie Mae injects capital into the household finance market two ways: by paying cash for mortgages issued by credit unions, banks, and other institutions and by purchasing pools of mortgages in return for mortgage-backed securities. To comply with Fannie Mae regulations, a loan must be under a certain amount. For instance, in 2005, Fannie Mae's upper limit on one-family loans was $359,650, up from $333,700 in 2004.

Fannie Mae holds around 12 percent of the mortgages in the United States. The rest are held by Freddie Mac, life insurance companies, pension funds, and various banks, credit unions, and other lending institutions.

Along with typical credit and financial analyst roles, secondary mortgage companies offer a variety of asset management and community development positions.

Mortgage Insurance

Conventional mortgage banking wisdom dictates that about 80 percent of a property's value can be recovered if a borrower defaults on a loan. To protect themselves against default, bankers would simply not authorize loans to people who had less than a 20 percent down payment on a home. To spur purchasing for the legions of cash-poor homebuyers, the industry created mortgage insurance. This had a democratizing effect on homeownership and is yet another factor contributing to the real estate run-up in recent years. Purchased by the homebuyer, it ensures lenders against loan defaults. Current legislation automatically cancels mortgage insurance once a borrower has amassed 20 percent equity in a property. Mortgage insurance typically costs borrowers from 0.35 percent to 1 percent of the loan premium. Leaders in the industry include the PMI Group, GE Mortgage Insurance, the Radian Group, and Mortgage Securities.

Underwriting/Real Estate Investment Banking

Perhaps the most interesting of finance options are the private funds that invest in real estate. These companies operate much like venture capitalists; they assemble a fund from institutional investors and wealthy individuals and invest opportunistically in real estate ventures. The companies that play in this arena are often the same ones that play in the sandboxes of asset management and investment banking. For them, real estate is simply a different asset class for investors. Goldman Sachs invests in real estate through its $2 billion Whitehall Street Real Estate Fund. Though the fund doesn't directly source, acquire, or manage property, it does use a subsidiary, the Archon Group, to perform those functions. Goldman isn't alone in this field. Asset management giant BlackRock invests in equity real estate through its Carbon Capital Fund. The Blackstone Group (no relation to BlackRock) has raised more than $6 billion in funds for investment in larger projects (more than $30 million) and real estate operating companies such as Hyatt Hotels, Host Marriott, and Berkshire Realty Group. Credit Suisse First Boston's DLJ Real Estate Capital Partners Funds manages private equity funds in excess of $1.9 billion.

Other Financing

Other financing in the real estate industry includes long-term lease agreements and commercial loans issued by commercial banks.

ANCILLARY SERVICES

Ancillary services act as the grease that keeps the cogs of the real estate industry from grinding to a halt. Services such as title searches, escrow, appraisal, and inspection build among market participants a sense of trust that allows, especially for consumers, their life savings to be handed over to complete strangers.

Title Search

A title search is the process of examining all of the relevant records of a property to confirm that the seller is the legal owner of a property and that there are no liens or other claims on the property.

Escrow

Simply defined, an escrow is a deposit of funds, a deed, or other instrument by one party for the delivery to another party upon completion of a particular condition or event. For example, in the case of purchasing a home, you set up an escrow account to hold your down payment until financing approval and property inspections are complete.

Appraisal

Appraisal is the art of valuing a property for insurance, taxation, and resale purposes. Appraisers find work in independent companies, larger brokerage and asset management firms, and government agencies.

Inspection and Warranty

Inspection and warranty are, as they sound, assurances by third parties that a property does not have any hidden problems such as termites, dry rot, or structural damage. In California, you can count on earthquake inspection and geology assessments to augment these reports. Typically, home sellers pay for such inspections.

CORPORATE REAL ESTATE

The bricks and mortar of bricks-and-mortar retailers rest on real estate, and lots of it. Retailers and old economy industrials devour real estate. The retail and industrial sectors are particularly land hungry and dwarf all but the largest REIT real estate investment companies. Wal-Mart, the country's largest retailer, owns and leases more than 590 million square feet of retail space in the United States, nearly triple the 202 million square feet controlled by Simon Property Group, the largest real estate company specializing in retail properties. Home Depot's more than 1,800 stores sit on some 200 million square feet of retail space. The industrial sector is just as impressive. In 2004, General Motors had a real estate portfolio of 300 million square feet, while Ford had 280 million square feet. The Boeing Corporation owns more than 120 million square feet of former military industrial complex that it acquired when it took over McDonnell Douglas. Boeing has set up a subsidiary real estate development group to improve the property; along with 777s and cruise missiles, Boeing is building office complexes.

Real estate is big business within these companies, with corresponding career opportunities. Corporate real estate officers are involved in the selection, development, and maintenance of sites. Site acquisition is a hugely strategic undertaking for retailers, and the role of acquisition analyst is therefore a prominent position within those companies. Other opportunities in corporate real estate include a microcosm of the positions found throughout the industry. For smaller corporations, the task of managing real estate is still enormous. Real estate directors in these companies manage relationships with property and building managers, negotiate with brokers, and articulate the needs of their business.

Industry Rankings

The following rankings represent some of the largest companies involved in the real estate industry as ranked by publicly reported or, in the case of private firms, estimated revenue.

Key Real Estate Companies

Company	2004 Revenue ($M)	1-Year Change (%)	Employees	Sector
Cendant Corp.	19,785	8.8	87,000	Diversified
Pulte Homes	11,711	29.4	13,000	Homebuilding
D.R. Horton	10,841	24.2	7,466	Homebuilding
Lennar Corp.	10,504	17.9	11,796	Homebuilding
The Trump Organization	10,400	22.4	22,000	Development
Centex Corp.	10,363	13.7	16,532	Homebuilding
KB Home	7,008	21.3	6,000	Homebuilding
Starwood Hotels & Resorts	5,368	42.0	120,000	REOC—hotels
NVR	4,250	15.6	4,407	Homebuilding
Hovnanian Enterprises	4,160	29.9	3,837	Homebuilding
M.D.C Holdings	4,009	37.3	3,600	Homebuilding
The Ryland Group	3,952	14.7	2,829	Homebuilding
Beazer Homes USA	3,907	23.0	3,428	Homebuilding
Toll Brothers	3,862	40.0	4,655	Homebuilding
Host Marriott	3,668	6.6	192	REIT—hospitality
Standard Pacific	3,355	42.1	2,100	Homebuilding
Equity Office Properties	3,305	−2.7	2,300	REIT—offices
Simon Property Group	2,722	13.0	4,610	REIT—retail mall
CB Richard Ellis Group	2,365	45.1	13,500	Commercial brokerage
Tishman Realty & Construction	2,195	10.8	900	Development

Key Real Estate Companies (cont'd)

Company	2004 Revenue ($M)	1-Year Change (%)	Employees	Sector
Meritage Homes	2,040	38.7	1,200	Homebuilding
Vornado Realty Trust	1,983	22.8	2,592	REIT—diversified
Equity Residential	1,898	3.4	6,000	REIT—multifamily
General Growth Properties	1,894	38.5	5,200	REIT—retail mall
WCI Communities	1,832	25.7	3,500	Homebuilding
William Lyon Homes	1,822	102.9	910	Homebuilding
AIMCO	1,549	2.5	6,800	REIT—multifamily
Brookfield Properties	1,442	5.8	1,400*	REOC—office
Boston Properties	1,412	2.8	667	REIT—diversified
FelCor Lodging Trust	1,204	0.1	70	REIT—hospitality
Duke Realty Corp.	1,181	46.0	1,100	REIT—office
Archstone-Smith Trust	919	1.5	2,640	REIT—residential

*2003 numbers.
Sources: *Fortune*; Hoover's; Crain's New York Business; WetFeet analysis.

Ten Largest Public REITs

REIT	2004 Revenue ($M)	1-Year Change (%)	Employees	Sector
Starwood Hotels & Resorts	5,368	42.0	120,000	Hotels
Host Marriott Corp.	3,668	6.6	192	Hotels
Equity Office Properties Trust	3,305	−2.7	2,300	Office
Simon Property Group	2,722	13.0	4,610	Retail/mall
Vornado Realty Trust	1,983	22.8	2,592	Diversified
Equity Residential Properties	1,898	3.4	6,000	Residential
General Growth Properties	1,894	38.5	5,200	Malls
AIMCO	1,549	2.5	6,800	Residential
Brookfield Properties Corp.	1,442	5.8	1,400*	Office
Boston Properties	1,412	2.8	667	Office

*2003 numbers.
Sources: National Association of Real Estate Investment Trusts; Hoover's; WetFeet analysis.

Leading Mortgage Originators

Originator	Loans Originated Q4 2004 ($M)	1-Year Change (%)
Countrywide Financial Corp.	95,315	24.9
Wells Fargo Home Mortgage	69,142	−3.4
Washington Mutual	59,003	−12.9
Chase Home Finance	44,433	−20.2
Bank of America	34,567	88.4

Sources: *National Mortgage News*; WetFeet analysis.

Industry Trends

The real estate industry has many sectors, and each of those has its own set of trends, which often conflict with the trends of other sectors. So, while not all trends cover the entire industry, they do shed light on where the industry and its constituent sectors appear to be headed. The following trends reflect our interviews with industry insiders as well as additional background research.

CAUTIOUS GANGBUSTERS: THE OUTLOOK

First quarter 2005 housing starts surged, hitting an all-time high for single family homes and showing impressive results for the multifamily sector as well, driven by an improving rental market and strong growth in condo development. Sales of new and existing homes were also solid. All of this bodes well for the homebuilding industry after prognostications that 2005 wouldn't match the strength of 2004. Interest rates, which are moving upward, had been expected to create a drag on demand, but growth in the GDP—and rising employment and household income—are a promising offset. D.R. Horton expects to sell 50,000 homes, an improvement on its impressive 2004 sales. Buying by investors and speculators, and a rise in adjustable-rate mortgages, could complicate the picture, along with the acceleration in the growth of housing prices that have led some analysts to forecast the bursting of the housing bubble. There are other signs a slowdown may take place, though perhaps not until 2006. *BusinessWeek* found that luxury homes declined in value in the last 3 months of 2004. A National Association of Realtors report that 36 percent of 2004's home sales were second homes, with 64 percent made as an investment, lends credence to the idea that the bubble may be getting bigger, however.

Commercial growth in 2005 promises an improvement over 2004, with multifamily dwellings expected to rise around 9 percent to $120 billion—topping the $112 billion spent at the peak of the dot-com boom in 2000. Expansion by retailers such as Lowe's and Wal-Mart, along with improving GDP, also bode well for the sector.

Office buildings appear to be rebounding as well, with the national vacancy rate dropping in 2004 and as much of 70 percent of new buildings being preleased. In 2005, 170 million square feet are expected to come available. Conditions do, of course, vary depending on the market. In Riverside and San Bernardino, for instance, vacancy rates hit just 9.5 percent in early 2005—better than New York City. San Mateo, in Silicon Valley, still recovering from the dot-com implosion, was at 27 percent.

EVERYMAN A DONALD TRUMP

REITs took real estate financing from back rooms and private investors to public markets. As the industry continues to grow into this model, real estate investments are becoming a more common addition to income earning investment portfolios, both in the public sector as REITS and as private equity for high-net-worth individuals. As stocks and other non–real estate equities have performed poorly, investors have poured even more money into real estate. With this newfound popularity, REITs and the real estate asset class are finding themselves to be the big man on the investment campus; and with this trend, increasingly more real estate finance should take place through public markets and investment houses. Of course, some analysts worry that a stock market recovery will spur an outflow of funds from real estate investments, and the consensus among analysts is that the portfolio-floating returns of the last several years can't and won't continue.

A SENSE OF SECURITIZATION

REITs have transformed the industry by making real estate investment transparent. An industry that was once characterized by backroom dealings is now largely defined by professional management and government oversight. This trend continues as REITs are increasing in number and becoming ever-larger investment vehicles subject to the same scrutiny as traditional securities.

ACCOUNTING ISSUES CONTINUE TO SPREAD TO OTHER INDUSTRIES

In spring 2005, Congress took up discussions about strengthening oversight of Fannie Mae and Freddie Mac, in response to accounting scandals expected to result in an $11 billion restatement of earnings for Fannie Mae and $5 billion for Freddie Mac. Created to help make homes affordable to homebuyers, Fannie Mae and Freddie Mac have issued some $1.8 trillion in debt, held by many of America's biggest financial institutions. Accounting issues, some fear, could create a problematic ripple effect through the entire economy.

BOOMERS CRASH INTO RETIREMENT

The aging of Baby Boomers presents a tectonic shift in real estate needs. As Boomers near retirement, many are snapping up second homes that will serve as nests in which to spend their golden years. The effect of this land rush is that prices of vacation homes in attractive markets are skyrocketing. Similarly, as Boomers sever cords with their working lives, they are apt to leave a glut of housing in the cities that they once called home.

FINDING A NICHE

Although the real estate industry has always been attuned to location (say it with us: location, location, location), it hasn't cared what the people in a location want. Companies are now taking more care to market to socioeconomic groups and anticipate the needs of different markets. The industry trend has manifested itself in the form of firms that cater exclusively to particular groups and through the trend of homebuilders in developing "mass customized" homes with luxury options like kitchen islands or high-end appliances available much in the same way car manufacturers offer rich Corinthian leather interiors and air conditioning for a premium.

IT'S A LITTLE EASIER BEING GREEN

Though the real estate industry is hardly considered a tree hugger, there is a major trend toward environmentally sensitive projects. To an extent, wealthy consumers also tend to be eco-conscious ones, pushing homebuilders and developers in an ecologically sensitive direction. Moreover, local, state, and federal legislation has necessitated such construction. Many new developments are "brown fields" projects, which take former industrial sites and make them into residential or office space.

The significance of the trend is where these projects are happening; rather than in hippy communes, today's sustainable development is taking place in the heart of corporate America. The Condé Nast building in Times Square in New York City has solar panels affixed to its roof. And architect William McDonough has built a practice around environmentally sensitive buildings, what he has termed "cradle to cradle" design. His work includes the revitalization of the Ford Motor Company's historic River Rouge complex, which has a roof completely covered in sod.

SQUEEZED IN THE MIDDLE

While large companies and small specialty firms will survive, industry experts predict that midsize companies will suffer. This is due in part to the increased costs of technology and infrastructure, which a high-touch small firm doesn't need, but a midsize firm doesn't have the economy of scale to make pay off. It's also due in part to the popularity of REITs, which need to be large to participate in public markets—as REITs grow, they swallow up midsize companies. Therefore, the fate of many a midsize company is one of two things: go out of business or get eaten by a predator.

WALL STREET IS LIKE LITHIUM

In former years, the real estate industry was like your brilliant, but manic-depressive friend, with higher highs, and lower lows. The cyclical nature of the industry was exacerbated by many small-time speculators who worked independent of one another. Developers tended to work with private capital and build on gut feel rather than sound analysis. The consequence was horrible overdevelopment during booms that led to overcapacity in lean years—a true boom-and-bust industry. As financial markets have taken over much of the financing of commercial development through REITs and private equity placement, they have also forced discipline on developers. Consequently, developers, now under Wall Street's scrutiny, have forced themselves to be much more disciplined—developments and property acquisitions are subject to sensitivity analysis and "what if" scenarios rather than wild hare speculation.

Picking and Choosing

RESIDENTIAL VS. COMMERCIAL

The biggest schism in the real estate industry is that found between the residential and commercial sides of the fence. Most of the opportunities in residential real estate are in the areas of sales, brokerage, and mortgage banking. Though the residential side of things offers rubber band–like flexibility—you are often your own boss—jobs in residential real estate don't allow for easy crossover into jobs in the commercial sector. On the other hand, commercial real estate has a vast universe of careers, many of which are transferable. Because REITs and asset managers need to perform brokerage and property management functions, commercial brokers and property managers can find jobs in the development and acquisition sector.

LOCATION

Real estate's old saw, "location, location, location," also applies to jobs in the real estate industry. Pick your location carefully when looking at a real estate career. You'll find that the market knowledge and industry contacts you build will be somewhat limited by location. Exceptions to this rule are careers in home building and real estate finance. To keep moving forward in the industry, you'll need to stay put. Moreover, location determines your profit potential. Because brokerage jobs are commission- and volume-driven, your bank account is going to get a lot fatter in regions that have high property values and commercial rent, as well as ones where a lot of new home buying and office space leasing is taking place. Manhattan or San Francisco will offer a greater reward potential than Muskogee, Oklahoma, for example.

COMPANY SIZE

The size of companies in the real estate industry varies dramatically, from Fortune 500 companies with thousands of employees, to niche developers and acquisition specialists with a handful of employees. Real estate is filled with big egos—so choose carefully. If you are in a small firm, you're likely to often feel the heat of being a partner. The flip side to this is that a small firm gives you the opportunity to learn the tricks from the masters themselves. Additionally, you'll get the opportunity to get let in on deals far sooner in a small company.

The Companies

The 30 profiles in this chapter focus on the largest companies in the real estate industry based on 2004 revenue, as well as several of the larger private players that go unranked. (See the "Industry Rankings" section in the previous chapter for more ranking information.) We include them to portray, in broad strokes, the larger panorama of the real estate industry.

APARTMENT INVESTMENT AND MANAGEMENT COMPANY (AIMCO)

4582 S. Ulster Street Parkway, Suite 1100
Denver, CO 80237
Phone: 303-757-8101
Ticker: AIV
www.aimco.com

AIMCO got its start in 1975, when Terry Considine founded The Considine Company (TCC). TCC acquired a majority stake in McDermott, Stein, and Ira in 1987, operating as Property Asset Management before Considine and Steve Ira decided to organize an apartment REIT—AIMCO. Today, if you go by units, AIMCO is the largest owner of apartments in the United States, with more than 280,000 units on 1,600 properties. AIMCO's reach extends to 47 states plus Washington, D.C., and Puerto Rico. For AIMCO, the money is in low-rent housing—the company has a unit that specializes in HUD-subsidized housing—and down-market properties.

Key Numbers

	2004	2003	1-Year Change (%)
Worldwide revenue ($M)	1,549	1,511	2.5
Worldwide earnings ($M)	264	159	65.9
Employees	6,800	7,300	−6.8

Sources: Hoover's; WetFeet analysis.

Recent Milestones

2005   Purchased Palazzo East luxury apartment complex in Los Angeles for $199 million—giving it 32 properties and more than 9,200 units in Southern California.

2004   Purchases Palazzo Park in Los Angeles for $163 million.

        Creates a new division, University Communities, to focus on properties that serve primarily college students.

2003   Becomes part of the S&P 500.

ARCHSTONE-SMITH TRUST

9200 E. Panorama Circle, Suite 400

Englewood, CO 80112

Phone: 303-708-5959

Ticker: ASN

www.archstonesmith.com

Archstone-Smith's empire consists of more than 88,000 garden-style and high-rise apartments on some 250 properties. Archstone's holdings are focused around markets in California, Florida, Seattle, Boston, Chicago, and Washington, D.C. *Fortune* recognized Archstone as one of "America's Most Admired Companies" in 2004, and *Colorado Biz Magazine* named it "Company of the Year."

Key Numbers

	2004	2003	1-Year Change (%)
Worldwide revenue ($M)	919	906	1.5
Worldwide earnings ($M)	542	434	25.1
Employees	2,640	2,730	−3.3

Sources: Hoover's; WetFeet analysis.

Recent Milestones

2005   Signs agreement with Oakwood Worldwide, the largest global provider of corporate housing, to acquire 30 apartment communities representing more than 10,000 units at a cost of $1.4 billion.

2004   Acquires 623-unit apartment complex in Los Angeles for $87 million and 254-unit building in Manhattan for $125 million.

2003   Sells its Consolidated Engineering Services subsidiary and its property management business.

BEAZER HOMES USA, INC.

1000 Abernathy Road, Suite 1200
Atlanta, GA 30328
Phone: 770-829-3700
Ticker: BZH
www.beazer.com

Targeting the middle-class buyer, Beazer operates in 40 markets in 22 states covering the Southeast, Mid-Atlantic, Midwest, West, and Central United States. Beazer Mortgage originates mortgages and Homebuilders Title Services provides title insurance services in select cities. Recognizing constraints on land and housing supply, Beazer's strategy is to use its size, scale, and capabilities to increase profitability through product expansion and offering different priced homes to leverage its national brand—and as the nation's sixth largest homebuilder, with a 23 percent increase in revenue in 2004 over 2003, it appears to be succeeding quite well.

Key Numbers

	2004	2003	1-Year Change (%)
Worldwide revenue ($M)	3,907	3,177	23.0
Worldwide earnings ($M)	236	173	36.5
Employees	3,428	2,986	14.8

Sources: Hoover's; WetFeet analysis.

Recent Milestones

2005   Announces record backlog for the quarter ended December 31, 2004, with 8,427 homes at a value of $2.35 billion.

2004   Reports a record 16,451 home closings and a 23 percent year-over-year increase in annual revenue.

2002   Acquires Crossman Communities.

BOSTON PROPERTIES, INC.

111 Huntington Avenue
Boston, MA 02199
Phone: 617-236-3300
Ticker: BXP
www.bostonproperties.com

Boston Properties, Mort Zuckerman's real estate venture, controls more than 40 million square feet of office space in its hometown of Boston as well as in San Francisco, New York City, and Washington, D.C. (Zuckerman also owns the *New York Daily News* and *U.S. News and World Reports.*) The company's marquee properties include the Embarcadero Center in San Francisco and Boston's Prudential Center.

The company is, properly, an UPREIT, an umbrella partnership real estate investment trust. Boston Properties L.P., which operates under the UPREIT, buys and sells properties and carries out operations. The company's portfolio consisted of 125 properties and 44.1 million square feet, including three properties under construction, at the end of 2004.

Key Numbers

	2004	2003	1-Year Change (%)
Worldwide revenue ($M)	1,412	1,373	2.8
Worldwide earnings ($M)	284	365	−22.3
Employees	667	662	0.8

Sources: Hoover's; WetFeet analysis.

Recent Milestones

2004   Forms Boston Properties Office Value-Added Fund, a strategic partnership to pursue acquisition in noncore office assets within the company's existing markets.

Raises $300 million in a public offering.

Completes its Times Square Tower project in Manhattan.

BROOKFIELD PROPERTIES CORPORATION

Corporate Headquarters:
BCE Place
181 Bay Street, Suite 330
Toronto, Ontario M5J 2T3, Canada
Phone: 416-369-2300
Ticker: BPO
www.brookfieldproperties.com

Primary U.S. Office:
1 Liberty Plaza
165 Broadway, 6th Floor
New York, NY 10006
Phone: 212-417-7000

Along with Bryan Adams, Mike Myers, and Celine Dion, Canada's exports to the United States include Brookfield Properties. The company operates primarily in the commercial sector; it spun off its residential unit, Brookfield Homes, in 2003. Brookfield is a subsidiary of Canadian mining company Brascan. Among the most famous of its 50 office properties in the United States and Canada are its New York City holdings at One, Two, and Four World Financial Center and One Liberty Plaza. The company's portfolio includes 46 commercial properties and development sites totaling more than 46 million square feet.

Key Numbers

	2004	2003	1-Year Change (%)
Worldwide revenue ($M)	1,442	1,363	5.8
Worldwide earnings ($M)	242	279	−13.3
Employees	n/a	1,400	7.7

Sources: Hoover's; WetFeet analysis.

Recent Milestones

2004   Acquires 801 Ninth Street NW, Potomac Tower, and Edison Place, to gain a foothold in the Washington, D.C., market.

Completes the Hudson's Bay Centre development in Toronto.

2003   Spins off Brookfield Homes.

CB RICHARD ELLIS GROUP, INC. (CBRE)

865 Figueroa Street, Suite 3400
Los Angeles, CA 90017
Phone: 213-613-3226
Ticker: CBG
www.cbre.com

Once the largest commercial brokerage in the country, CBRE got even bigger when it acquired Insignia Financial in 2003, and it now bills itself as a full-service real estate company. The company's picnic basket of products includes market research, real estate brokerage, mortgage banking, and asset management and advisory services. Richard Blum, the husband of U.S. Senator Dianne Feinstein, holds a 43 percent stake in CBRE. The company has a broader international scope than most firms, with Europe, the Middle East, and Africa accounting for a significant portion of annual sales.

Key Numbers

	2004	2003	1-Year Change (%)
Worldwide revenue ($M)	2,365	1,630	45.1
Worldwide earnings ($M)	65	−35	n/a
Employees	13,500	13,500	0

Sources: Hoover's; WetFeet analysis.

Recent Milestones

2005   Brett White, formerly the company's president, succeeds Ray Wirta as CEO.

2004   The company offers shares of CBRE in an IPO, raising nearly $140 million.

Named one of the "Best Places to Work" by *Atlanta* magazine.

2003   Merges with commercial real estate broker Insignia Financial.

CENDANT CORPORATION

9 W. 57th Street
New York, NY 10019
Phone: 212-413-1800
Ticker: CD
www.cendant.com

Cendant has risen substantially since CEO Walter Forbes was indicted for cooking the company books and fabricating $500 million in profits in 1997. The books have cooled, and Cendant has become a franchise giant; real estate franchises and operations represented close to 30 percent of revenue in 2004. Cendant's portfolio includes such diverse companies as Avis, Cheap Tickets, and Progeny Marketing. Though only about 20 percent of its revenue streams through real estate holdings, Cendant is one of the country's largest residential real estate brokers and hotel franchisers. The company's real estate operations include 200,000 sales associates working under the Century 21, Coldwell Banker, Coldwell Banker Commercial, ERA, and NRT brands. Cendant leverages this market presence with Cendant Mortgage, an inbound telemarketer-based mortgage loan originator.

The company's hotel holdings include time-share giant RCI, Fairfield Resorts, and a slew of hotel chains that dot America's interstate off-ramps and touch the cockles of countless vacationers: Ramada, Days Inn, Travelodge, Super 8, Howard Johnson, Wingate, Knights Inn, Amerihost Inn, Holiday Cottages group, and Villager.

Key Numbers

	2004	2003	1-Year Change (%)
Worldwide revenue ($M)	19,785	18,192	8.8
Worldwide earnings ($M)	2,082	1,172	77.6
Employees	87,000	87,000	0

Sources: Hoover's; WetFeet analysis.

Recent Milestones

2005   Spins off its mortgage and fleet management businesses into a wholly owned subsidiary, PHH Corporation, and announces mortgage venture with PHH to begin operating in mid-2005.

2004   Sells its 15 Sotheby's International Realty offices.

2002   Buys TRUST International from Bertelsmann.

Acquires Budget Rent A Car parent Budget Group for $110 million and Novasol AS, a European vacation rental company.

CENTEX CORPORATION

2728 N. Harwood Street

Dallas, TX 75201

Phone: 214-981-5000

Ticker: CTX

www.centex.com

With annual revenue of more than $10 billion, Sunbelt-based Centex is one of the largest homebuilders in the country, with some 400,000 homes completed. Operating in 90 metropolitan markets and 26 states as well as in the United Kingdom, Centex's CTX mortgage division finances mortgages, 70 percent of which go to loans for the parent company's houses. The company also operates insurance and title businesses, runs a construction company, and owns investment real estate businesses.

Key Numbers

	2004	2003	1-Year Change (%)
Worldwide revenue ($M)	10,364	9,117	13.7
Worldwide earnings ($M)	828	556	48.9
Employees	16,532	17,540	−5.7

Sources: *Fortune*; Hoover's; WetFeet analysis.

Recent Milestones

2005 Ranks number one in its industry in *Fortune* magazine's annual "America's Most Admired Companies" list.

2004 Spins off Centex Construction Products, which then becomes Eagle Materials.

Ranks among top-10 U.S. homebuilders yet again—the only company to do so for more than 30 consecutive years, according to *Professional Builder* magazine.

2003 Spins off Cavco, its manufactured home business.

Acquires St. Louis and Indianapolis regional homebuilder, The Jones Company.

D.R. HORTON, INC.

301 Commerce Street
Fort Worth, TX 76102
Phone: 817-390-9200
Ticker: DHI
www.drhorton.com

Founded in 1978 by Donald R. Horton, D.R. Horton is one of America's largest homebuilders. It specializes in the single-family, entry-level, and move-up markets, though it also builds luxury homes. By the end of 2005, it expects to sell 50,000 homes. Its 51 divisions build in 63 markets covering 21 states, with its heaviest presence in the West, Southwest, and Southeast. Along with homes, D.R. Horton provides mortgage and title insurance.

Key Numbers

	2004	2003	1-Year Change (%)
Worldwide revenue ($M)	10,841	8,727	24.2
Worldwide earnings ($M)	975	626	55.8
Employees	7,466	6,348	17.6

Sources: Hoover's; WetFeet analysis.

Recent Milestones

2005   Reports a contract backlog of 17,405 homes and 31 percent increase in net sales during the first quarter of the fiscal year.

Moves its headquarters from Arlington, Texas, to Forth Worth.

2004   Becomes the first homebuilder to build more than 45,000 homes in a single fiscal year.

DUKE REALTY CORPORATION

600 E. 96th Street, Suite 100
Indianapolis, IN 46240
Phone: 317-808-6000
Ticker: DRE
www.dukerealty.com

Duke's kingdom consists of suburban office space in the Midwest and South. As if the geography it operates in weren't glitzy enough, consider this: Nearly three-fourths of its holdings are warehouses, with offices rounding out the other 25 percent. The company is sitting on more than 4,500 acres of undeveloped land. Duke's interests include construction, asset management, and leasing services divisions.

Key Numbers

	2004	2003	1-Year Change (%)
Worldwide revenue ($M)	1,181	809	46
Worldwide earnings ($M)	189	199	−5.3
Employees	1,100	1,011	8.8

Sources: Hoover's; WetFeet analysis.

Recent Milestones

2005   Announces $68 million in fourth quarter dispositions from 2004, $81 million in new developments, and $80 million in third-party construction starts.

2004   Acquires 57 acres in Frisco, Texas, for development of up to 900,000 square feet of office space.

2003   Amasses $50 million in second quarter development investments.

EQUITY OFFICE PROPERTIES TRUST

2 N. Riverside Plaza, Suite 2100
Chicago, IL 60606
Phone: 312-466-3300
Ticker: EOP
www.equityoffice.com

"Grave Dancer" Sam Zell pioneered the REIT industry, and made a fortune in the process by buying up distressed properties after the real estate crash of the early 1990s and funding his spree through public equity markets. This industry-defining act gave birth to Equity Office Properties Trust, the largest public REIT in the country and the nation's largest office building owner and manager.

The firm's property arsenal includes more than 124 million square feet of office space in 700 properties in 32 metropolitan areas. Sales of nearly $2 billion of office properties, 7 percent of its portfolio, raise questions about its ability to cover its dividend—though take advantage of a hot real estate market. Zell's other scion, Equity Residential Property Trust, is the largest multifamily REIT, with nearly $2 billion in annual revenue and 250,000 housing units.

Key Numbers

	2004	2003	1-Year Change (%)
Worldwide revenue ($M)	3,305	3,397	–2.7
Worldwide earnings ($M)	137	655	–79.1
Employees	2,300	2,400	–4.2

Sources: Hoover's; WetFeet analysis.

Recent Milestones

2005   Buys Verizon's choice headquarters on Sixth Avenue and 42nd Street in New York City for more than $500 million, winning the bidding over Brookfield Properties, Reckson Associates, and Trizec Properties.

Sells 12 offices totaling 1 million square feet in suburban Philadelphia for $159 million, essentially exiting the Philadelphia market.

2004   Sells $177 million in assets, including 1.3 million square feet of office space.

EQUITY RESIDENTIAL

2 N. Riverside Plaza, Suite 450
Chicago, IL 60606
Phone: 312-474-1300
Ticker: EQR
www.equityapartments.com

The largest apartment owner by sales (but not volume), Sam Zell's Equity Residential owns some 223,500 apartment units in about 1,000 properties throughout 33 states. While the residential rental market has not been as hot as other real estate sectors, Equity Residential has managed to maintain steady earnings, and rising interest rates could lead to a stronger performance in 2005 and 2006. Over the past 3 years, Equity Residential has sold some $2.7 billion in properties and replaced them with newer properties in markets it considers more strategic—the company prefers properties from 1990 or newer. Zell started Equity Residential in 1969, and took the company public in 1993. Since then, the company has issued multiple offerings to investors hoping to cash in on Zell's magic.

Key Numbers

	2004	2003	1-Year Change (%)
Worldwide revenue ($M)	1,898	1,834	3.4
Worldwide earnings ($M)	472	544	−13.1
Employees	6,000	6,000	0.0

Sources: Hoover's; WetFeet analysis.

Recent Milestones

2005   Announces that President and CEO Bruce Duncan will step down at year's end and be replaced by David Neighecut, the chief financial officer and top strategist.

2003   The company sells $1.2 billion of assets in secondary and tertiary markets.

2002   Purchases and, later that year, sells Globe Business Resources, an office and residential furniture seller.

FELCOR LODGING TRUST INCORPORATED

545 E. John Carpenter Freeway, Suite 1300
Irving, TX 75062
Phone: 972-444-4900
Ticker: FCH
www.felcor.com

FelCor is the second-largest hotel REIT in the country, with 40,000 rooms in 142 hotels in 32 states and Canada. Intercontinental Hotels holds a 17 percent stake in the company. FelCor's strategy is to buy, renovate, and rebrand properties to one of its existing brands. FelCor brands include Embassy Suites, Crowne Plaza, Sheraton, Holiday Inn, Westin, and Doubletree. The company outsources management of its hotels to Starwood, Hilton, and Intercontinental.

Key Numbers

	2004	2003	1-Year Change (%)
Worldwide revenue ($M)	1,204	1,203	0.1
Worldwide earnings ($M)	–100	–310	n/a
Employees	70	66	6.1

Sources: Hoover's; WetFeet analysis.

Recent Milestones

2005   Plans to offer 5.4 million depositary shares to raise $135 million.

2004   Sells properties in Texas, Mississippi, and Nebraska for $30 million and purchases Holiday Inn in Santa Monica, California.

2003   Sells "nonstrategic" assets worth $12.1 million, including a Hampton Inn and parking lot.

GENERAL GROWTH PROPERTIES

110 N. Wacker Drive
Chicago, IL 60606
Phone: 312-960-5000
Ticker: GGP
www.generalgrowth.com

General Growth Properties is all about growth—especially after its 2004 acquisition of The Rouse Company, which added 37 regional shopping malls, four community centers, and six mixed-use projects. This followed the 2002 acquisition of JP Realty, which added 18 regional malls and 26 community centers to its portfolio. Today, General Growth operates some 200 regional shopping malls and 200 million square feet of property, making it the second-largest owner/operator of malls after Simon Property Group.

Key Numbers

	2004	2003	1-Year Change (%)
Worldwide revenue ($M)	1,894	1,270	38.5
Worldwide earnings ($M)	267.9	263.4	1.7
Employees	5,200	3,850	35.1

Sources: Hoover's; WetFeet analysis.

Recent Milestones

2004   Buys The Rouse Company in a $7.2 billion deal, adding 40 million square feet; occupancy for acquired properties is 92 percent.

Sells nonretail assets obtained in the JP Realty acquisition for $67 million.

HOST MARRIOTT CORPORATION

6903 Rockledge Drive, Suite 1500
Bethesda, MD 20817
Phone: 240-744-1000
Ticker: HMT
www.hostmarriott.com

The legacy of the J.W. Marriott hotel empire, Host Marriott Corporation owns Marriott, Ritz-Carlton, Four Seasons, Swissôtel, and Hyatt hotels, while fellow offspring Marriott International manages them. The Marriott family still owns nearly 10 percent of the company. Organized as an REIT in 1999, Host Marriott edged out Hospitality Property Corporation as the largest hotel REIT. Today, Marriott invests in premier properties in prime locations; its 107 hotels and approximately 54,000 rooms are in downtown, suburban, airport, and resort locations. Most of its properties are branded as Ritz-Carlton or Marriott hotels.

Key Numbers

	2004	2003	1-Year Change (%)
Worldwide revenue ($M)	3,668	3,442	6.6
Worldwide earnings ($M)	0	14	n/a
Employees	192	182	5.5

Sources: Hoover's; WetFeet analysis.

Recent Milestones

2005   Sells six smaller hotels to fund future acquisitions of larger, luxury hotels.

2004   Purchases the Fairmont Kea Lani Maui for $355 million.

HOVNANIAN ENTERPRISES, INC.

10 Highway 35
Red Bank, NJ 07701
Phone: 732-747-7800
Ticker: HOV
www.khov.com

Founded by Kevork S. Hovnanian in 1959 and in its second generation of family leadership, K. Hovnanian Homes includes townhomes, condominiums, and detached single-family homes for first-time, move-up, and luxury buyers. Recognized as one of the 100 fastest growing companies by *Fortune* in 2004, Hovnanian delivers more than 14,500 homes a year in 16 states, marketing and selling under names that include K. Hovnanian Homes, Goodman Homes, Matzel & Mumford, Diamond Homes, Westminister Homes, and Forecast Homes.

Key Numbers

	2004	2003	1-Year Change (%)
Worldwide revenue ($M)	4,160	3,202	29.9
Worldwide earnings ($M)	348.7	257.4	35.5
Employees	3,837	3,249	18.1

Sources: Hoover's; WetFeet analysis.

Recent Milestones

2005   Buys Cambridge Homes, a Central Florida builder, which built 599 homes in Central Florida in 2004, with a 486-house backlog and 3,600 building lots.

Acquires Town & Country Homes, ranked as the 52nd largest builder nationally in 2004 by *Builder Magazine*, strengthening the firm's position in the Chicago and Florida markets.

2004   Acquires Rocky Gorge Homes in McLean, Virginia.

2003   Acquires Brighton Homes in Houston and Great Western Homes in Tampa, Florida.

THE IRVINE COMPANY INC.

550 Newport Center Drive
Newport Beach, CA 92658
Phone: 949-720-2000
Ownership: private
www.irvinecompany.com

The Irvine Company is, at heart, a ranch. James Irvine started the company in 1864 as a 120,000-acre ranch. Of course, the ranch happened to comprise nearly one quarter of Orange County's entire area. In the early 1960s, the company developed a master plan for a series of communities around which a good portion of Orange County grew. The company still owns nearly 45,000 acres. Nearly 240,000 people live on The Irvine Ranch. Along with residential housing, the ranch incorporates office space, including the Irvine Spectrum, as well as golf courses, marinas, and other amenities you'd expect to find in sunny Southern California. In 1985, the company started the Irvine Spectrum, a 5,000-acre high-tech industrial park designed to reap the benefits of California's technology boom. The company followed up on this strategy by purchasing property in Silicon Valley.

Note: As a private company, The Irvine Company releases limited financial and personnel data.

Recent Milestones

2004   Launches $45 million reinvestment program in its office portfolio.

2003   Donates to the public a 42-acre parcel called Moro Ridge Link that connects the Cleveland National Forest, California's southernmost National Forest, to the Pacific Coast.

KB HOME

10990 Wilshire Boulevard, 7th Floor
Los Angeles, CA 90024
Phone: 310-231-4000
Ticker: KBH
www.kbhome.com

The original wealth vehicle for art collector and philanthropist billionaire Eli Broad, KB Home runs hot in the Sunbelt. KB Home has expanded its reach outside of California through the Southwest and on to Florida over the past 10 years through acquisitions, most recently of Orlando-based American Heritage Homes and Atlanta-based Colony Homes. Today, KB Home operates in 392 communities catering to first-time and trade-up homebuyers with homes ranging from 1,200 to 3,900 square feet. Internationally, KB Home builds homes in France, which accounts for more than 14 percent of the firm's unit sales. As with other major homebuilders, KB Home operates a mortgage company to help its customers finance its homes. KB Home has innovated the home building process by letting buyers customize certain home features and by offering lease-to-own options.

Key Numbers

	2004	2003	1-Year Change (%)
Worldwide revenue ($M)	7,008	5,775	21.3
Worldwide earnings ($M)	481	371	29.7
Employees	6,000	5,100	17.6

Sources: Hoover's; WetFeet analysis.

Recent Milestones

2005   Announces a 65 percent jump in profits for the first quarter.

2004   Gains a toehold in the Southeast with the purchase of South Carolina–based Palmetto Traditional Homes.

2003   Acquires Chicago-based Zale Homes for $33 million and Atlanta-based Colony Homes.

LEFRAK ORGANIZATION INC.

9777 Queens Boulevard
Rego Park, NY 11374
Phone: 718-459-9021
Ownership: private
www.lefrak.com

The Lefrak Organization plays second chair only to Donald Trump in the New York area. A family-controlled dynasty, the Lefrak Organization has been building residential and commercial real estate in New York and New Jersey for more than 100 years. The company owns 71,000 housing units in the metropolitan New York area and manages an additional 40,000. Along with the well-known Battery Park City development, the 5,000-unit behemoth Lefrak City in Queens, developments in Jersey City, and projects on Long Island, the Lefrak portfolio includes subsidiaries Lefrak Oil and Gas and Lefrak Entertainment.

Note: As a private company, the Lefrak Organization releases limited financial and personnel data.

Recent Milestones

2004   Named the country's sixth-largest apartment owner by *National Real Estate Investor* magazine.

2003   Initiates plans to open up an office outside of metro New York for the first time in its history.

LENNAR CORPORATION

700 NW 107th Avenue
Miami, FL 33172
Phone: 305-559-4000
Ticker: LEN
www.lennar.com

Lennar, whose name is derived from the names of founders Leonard Miller and Alfred Rosen, cut its teeth in the home-building business in Miami in the 1950s. The company acquired U.S. Home and The Fortress Group to strengthen its presence outside Florida. With more than 500,000 homes in its tool belt, Lennar, along with Centex and Pulte homes, is now one of the leading homebuilders in the United States. Like Centex, Lennar operates a financial services business—mortgage, title, closing—to get people into its homes.

The company operates in 16 states and builds homes ranging from $100,000 to more than $1 million under such brands as Lennar, Village Builders, Winncrest Homes, Renaissance Homes, Greystone Homes, NuHome, U.S. Home, Orrin Thompson, Lundgren Bros., and Rutenberg Homes.

Though public, the company remains closely held: CEO Stuart Miller, son of founder Leonard Miller, owns 65 percent of the company.

Key Numbers

	2004	2003	1-Year Change (%)
Worldwide revenue ($M)	10,505	8,908	17.9
Worldwide earnings ($M)	946	751	25.8
Employees	11,796	10,572	11.6

Sources: Hoover's; WetFeet analysis.

Recent Milestones

2004 First quarter profits jump 39 percent over year-prior, with average sale prices of homes jumping from $256,000 to $292,000.

   Acquires San Antonio–based Connell-Barron Homes; Jacksonville, Florida–based Classic American Homes; and Newhall Land and Farming Company, a builder of master planned communities.

2003 Acquires Seppala Homes, Coleman Homes, and Mid America Title Company, increasing its presence in South Carolina, Central California, and Chicago, respectively.

M.D.C. HOLDINGS, INC.

3600 S. Yosemite Street, Suite 900
Denver, CO 80237
Phone: 303-773-1100
Ticker: MDC
www.richmondamerican.com

Colorado's top homebuilder is also a major player in suburban Maryland, Las Vegas, Salt Lake City, and Phoenix and Tucson—and it's growing in Jacksonville and California, among other places. M.D.C. Holdings operates as Richmond American Homes and includes within the family HomeAmerica Mortgage Corporation, providing mortgage financing primarily for Richmond homebuyers; American Home Title Company; and American Home Insurance.

Larry A. Mizel, who founded the company in 1972, is chairman and chief executive officer.

Key Numbers

	2004	2003	1-Year Change (%)
Worldwide revenue ($M)	4,009	2,920	37.3
Worldwide earnings ($M)	391	212	84.4
Employees	3,600	2,800	28.6

Sources: Hoover's; WetFeet analysis.

Recent Milestones

2005   In the first quarter, announces orders for 4,546 homes—highest in the company's history—along with a record backlog of 7,893 homes.

Acquires rights to 1,200 finished lots in California from Del Valle Homes.

2002   Announces goal of doubling its size within 5 years.

NVR, INC.

7601 Lewinsville Road, Suite 300
McLean, VA 22102
Phone: 717-761-2000
Ticker: NVR
www.nvrinc.com

NVR operates in two business segments—homebuilding and mortgage banking. The homebuilding brands, which operate in 18 metropolitan areas in 11 states, include Ryan Homes, which has constructed nearly 200,000 homes for first-time and move-up buyers since its founding in 1948; NVHomes, which caters to upscale homebuyers; and Fox Ridge Homes, Nashville's largest homebuilder. NVR Mortgage offers financing programs and settlement and title services from 16 branches in areas where NVR builds homes.

Key Numbers

	2004	2003	1-Year Change (%)
Worldwide revenue ($M)	4,250	3,678	15.6
Worldwide earnings ($M)	523	420	24.6
Employees	4,407	3,850	14.4

Sources: Hoover's; WetFeet analysis.

Recent Milestones

2005   Announces that 2005 net income will exceed 2004 net income by 15 percent during the first quarter, provided housing activity stays at current levels.

2004   Operating income from mortgage banking declines 12 percent over 2003, while new home orders increase 4 percent.

PULTE HOMES, INC.

100 Bloomfield Hills Parkway, Suite 300
Bloomfield Hills, MI 48304
Phone: 248-647-2750
Ticker: PHM
www.pulte.com

With its acquisition of blue-hair community developer Del Webb in 2001, Pulte
Homes became the largest homebuilder of "active adult" communities in the country.
It built some 45,000 homes in 2004, raising the number of shelters the company has
erected in its lifetime to more than 408,000. Pulte operates in the Latin American
markets of Mexico and Puerto Rico. Like the other major homebuilders, Pulte has a
significant financial services and mortgage origination business to serve its homebuyers.
In addition to the senior living communities of Del Webb, Pulte builds a wide range of
entry-level and move-up homes ranging from $75,000 to more than $1 million.

Pulte's homebuilding success has translated into beefy returns for its investors;
BusinessWeek ranked Pulte as one of the 50 best-performing stocks of 2003 and 2004.

Key Numbers

	2004	2003	1-Year Change (%)
Worldwide revenue ($M)	11,711	9,049	29.4
Worldwide earnings ($M)	987	625	57.9
Employees	13,000	10,800	20.4

Sources: Hoover's; WetFeet analysis.

Recent Milestones

2005   Ranks 12th on the *BusinessWeek* 50.

2004   Sells off its Argentina operations to Grupo Farallon.

2003   Expands operations in Southern California with the purchase of ColRich Communities, and acquires Sivage-Thomas Homes, expanding its presence in New Mexico and Arizona.

Wins a judgment by U.S. Court of Federal Claims stating the company had been damaged by a breach of contract by the U.S. Government in 1988.

THE RYLAND GROUP, INC.

24025 Park Sorrento, Suite 400
Calabasas, CA 91302
Phone: 818-223-7500
Ticker: RYL
www.ryland.com

The Ryland Group hovers below the reigning junta of D.R. Horton, Pulte, Centex, Lennar, and KB Home in the league of the nation's largest homebuilders. Like the other homebuilders, Ryland posted impressive gains in 2004—with nearly 15 percent revenue growth and adding to its net income by close to a third. With a goal of sustainability and a focus on emerging and geographically diverse markets, Ryland's ambitions are more conservative than those of its peers. Ryland uses subcontractors for all construction in the 14 states in which it builds. Like other builders, Ryland offers a suite of financial services ranging from mortgage origination, title search, mortgage insurance, and escrow services to its buyers.

Key Numbers

	2004	2003	1-Year Change (%)
Worldwide revenue ($M)	3,952	3,444	14.7
Worldwide earnings ($M)	321	242	32.6
Employees	2,829	2,558	10.6

Sources: Hoover's; WetFeet analysis.

Recent Milestones

2004   New communities in Las Vegas open.

2003   Begins operating in California's Inland Empire, east of Los Angeles.

2002   CEO R. Chad Dreier inks employment agreement that gives him an annual base salary of $1 million through 2007.

SIMON PROPERTY GROUP, INC.

National City Center
115 West Washington Street, Suite 15
Indianapolis, IN 46204
Phone: 317-636-1600
Ticker: SPG
www.simon.com

The Simon Property Group has a simple strategy for making money in real estate: own malls. Simon is the largest shopping mall owner and one of the largest retail property owners and managers in the country. Simon has an interest in 296 properties throughout the United States, amounting to more than 202 million square feet of potentially revenue-generating space. Additionally, the company has holdings in 51 European shopping centers, five outlet centers in Japan, and one property each in Mexico and Canada.

Key Numbers

	2004	2003	1-Year Change (%)
Worldwide revenue ($M)	2,722	2,408	13.0
Worldwide earnings ($M)	450	482	−6.6
Employees	4,610	4,040	14.1

Sources: Hoover's; WetFeet analysis.

Recent Milestones

2005   St. Johns Town Center, a 1.5-million-square-foot open-air retail center in Jacksonville, Florida, opens in March.

2004   Purchases high-end outlet mall owner Chelsea Property Group for $1.3 billion.

2003   Unsuccessfully bids for Taubman Centers.

2002   Buys mall properties of Rodamco.

STARWOOD HOTELS & RESORTS WORLDWIDE, INC.

1111 Westchester Avenue
White Plains, NY 10604
Phone: 914-640-8100
Ticker: HOT
www.starwoodhotels.com

The stars come out for Starwood Hotels and Resorts, one of the largest hotel operators around. Technically organized as an REOC (real estate operating company), Starwood reached its lofty position when it acquired Westin Hotels, ITT, and Vistana in 1998 and 1999. Also in 1999, the company changed its structure from an REIT to an REOC, no longer requiring it to pay out 95 percent of its earnings as dividends. It has used this additional capital to build stellar brand-name hotels. The company runs primarily high-end and luxury hotels and includes tony brands such as Sheraton, Westin, W Hotels, Four Points, and St. Regis. Its subsidiary, Starwood Vacation Ownership, runs time-share properties.

Key Numbers

	2004	2003	1-Year Change (%)
Worldwide revenue ($M)	5,368	3,779	42.0
Worldwide earnings ($M)	395	309	27.8
Employees	120,000	110,000	9.1

Sources: Hoover's; WetFeet analysis.

Recent Milestones

2005   Announces plans to open more than 70 new hotels in 2005 and 2006.

2004   Acquires Bliss Spa chain from LVMH.

Steven Heyer replaces company founder Barry Sternlicht as CEO.

2003   Sells Italian Ciga assets to Colony Capital.

TISHMAN REALTY & CONSTRUCTION CO. INC.

666 Fifth Avenue
New York, NY 10103
Phone: 212-399-3600
Ownership: private
www.tishman.com

What started as Julius Tishman's tenement construction firm has become one of the country's largest real estate companies. Today, Tishman is not only involved in construction, but also acquisition and development, real estate services, hotels, and building technology. Counted among the company's high-profile construction projects are Disney's EPCOT Center, Madison Square Garden, the twin towers of the World Trade Center, and Chicago's Hancock Center. Operating unit Tishman Hotel Corporation owns and operates some 85 hotels with more than 30,000 rooms.

Key Numbers

	2004	2003	1-Year Change (%)
Worldwide revenue ($M)*	2,000	2,000	0
Worldwide earnings ($M)	n/a	n/a	n/a
Employees	900	900	0

*Estimated.
Sources: Hoover's; WetFeet analysis.

Recent Milestones

2004   Begins construction on 1,776-foot Freedom Tower on the site of the twin towers.

2002–1997
        Focuses on revitalization efforts around 42nd Street and Times Square; includes development of the Reuters America headquarters; the Condé Nast building, Tishman's E Walk (an entertainment center) and Westin Hotel, and ABC's "Good Morning America" building.

TOLL BROTHERS, INC.

250 Gilbraltar Road
Horsham, PA 19044
Phone: 215-938-8000
Ticker: TOL
www.tollbrothers.com

Toll Brothers likes to say it builds not homes, but communities. Operating in 21 states, its homes are primarily of the luxury variety; prices average about $500,000. Demand in 2005 looks solid: Profits doubled in the first quarter. It operates 10 communities for active adults over 55, some of which have Arnold Palmer Signature golf courses. Company subsidiaries offer insurance, home security, landscaping, and mortgage services, while partnerships with the National Wildlife Federation and Audubon Society have led to programs such as Backyard Wildlife Habitats and Audubon Cooperative Sanctuaries for Golf Courses.

Key Numbers

	2004	2003	1-Year Change (%)
Worldwide revenue ($M)	3,862	2,758	40.0
Worldwide earnings ($M)	409	260	57.5
Employees	4,655	3,416	36.3

Sources: Hoover's; WetFeet analysis.

Recent Milestones

2005   *Barron*'s names Chairman and CEO Robert I. Toll one of the world's 30 most respected CEOs.

Forbes names Toll Brothers to the Platinum 400 as one of "America's Best Managed Companies" for the fifth year in a row.

2004   Wins bid to purchase 1,940 acres in Henderson, Nevada.

2003   Acquires homebuilder Richard R. Dostie, Inc., and The Manhattan Building Company.

THE TRUMP ORGANIZATION

725 Fifth Avenue
New York, NY 10022
Phone: 212-832-2000
Ownership: private
www.trumponline.com

The largest real estate developer in the country, Donald Trump's eponymous organization owns some of Manhattan's most prestigious addresses. In addition to the landmark 40 Wall Street Building and General Motors Building, Trump owns a collection of sleek black residential monoliths that jut into the Manhattan skyline. One of these, the Trump World Tower, is the tallest residential building in the world. Off the island, Trump controls an interest in Trump Hotels and Casino Resorts, which owns a number of Atlantic City casinos and other hotels across the country. Trump is known for putting together partnership deals in which other investors pony up more capital while Trump retains control of the property.

The Trump Organization's penchant for marquee properties had the company at one time owning the Empire State Building and renovating Manhattan's famous Delmonico Hotel. The company's current prime time project is the Trump International Hotel & Tower Chicago. Trump's company, started in 1974 as an umbrella organization to cover the tycoon's various interests, also owns a 50 percent stake in the Miss Universe competition.

Key Numbers

	2004	2003	1-Year Change (%)
Worldwide revenue ($M)	10,400	8,500	22.4
Worldwide earnings ($M)	n/a	n/a	n/a
Employees	22,000	22,000	0.0

Note: As a private company, The Trump Organization releases only limited financial information.
Sources: *Crain's New York Business* 1/24/2005; Hoover's; WetFeet analysis.

Recent Milestones

2004   Puts landmark 40 Wall Street skyscraper on the market for approximately $520 million.

Purchases Hollinger International's interest in the Trump development on the Chicago riverfront, the former headquarters of the *Chicago Sun-Times*.

2003   Trump and partner Conseco, an insurance company, are forced to sell the General Motors Building as Conseco files for bankruptcy.

2002   Acquires and converts the Pre-War Delmonico Hotel into a luxury apartment house.

Begins work on $600 million Trump Grande Ocean Resort and Residences in Miami Beach, Florida.

VORNADO REALTY TRUST

888 7th Avenue
New York, NY 10019
Phone: 212-894-7000
Ticker: VNO
www.vno.com

Vornado has rocked the real estate world like a hurricane since it transformed itself from a retailer to a real estate company in 1981. Vornado, which started out as "Two Guys" discount furniture in 1948, now owns and manages approximately 87 million square feet, primarily in metropolitan New York and Washington, D.C. The company has holdings in three areas: office, retail, and trade show space. The company's New York Portfolio includes 20 office properties or approximately 13.5 million square feet of office space. Its Washington, D.C., holdings include 66 office properties and one hotel. In Chicago, it owns and manages the 8.6-million-square-foot Merchandise Mart. In addition to these core holdings, it has 94 retail properties in Puerto Rico, a 47 percent interest in AmeriCold Realty Trust, and a variety of other properties.

Key Numbers

	2004	2003	1-Year Change (%)
Worldwide revenue ($M)	1,983	1,614	22.8
Worldwide earnings ($M)	593	461	28.7
Employees	2,592	2,700	−4.0

Sources: Hoover's; WetFeet analysis.

Recent Milestones

2005   Announces plans to sell its share in 400 North LaSalle Residential Tower in Chicago for $126 million.

Acquires the retail condominium of the Westbury Hotel in Manhattan for $113 million.

Provides $450 in equity for a one-third interest in a joint venture that acquires Toys "R" Us.

2004   Acquires 25 supermarket properties worth $65 million.

On the Job

The Big Picture

Acquisition and Development

Brokerage and Sales

Property Management

Finance

Ancillary Services

Corporate Real Estate

Real People Profiles

The Big Picture

The real estate industry has a diverse range of positions for potential job seekers; as such, the job descriptions that follow are representative rather than exhaustive. Furthermore, the positions listed represent the range of career tracks as well as those that offer inroads to advancement. You should know that with this variety comes a nonuniform set of career opportunities. Not only do positions vary greatly in responsibility and remuneration, but also in their ability to serve as a platform for career mobility. For instance, jobs in commercial brokerage or project management positions in development companies serve as good bases to learn the industry and are established stepping-stones. Other positions, such as those in appraisal, don't afford such mobility. You should also keep in mind that there is a significant rift between commercial and residential real estate, with few bridges—notably in finance and development—between the two. If you decide to go to work in the commercial or residential sectors, you'll find that it might be difficult to cross the fence to the other field. After all, the skills you gain on one side will not necessarily translate to the other.

Professionals attain much of their functional knowledge on the job; therefore many of the positions in the industry don't require set educational or industry backgrounds. Exceptions include analyst positions that require solid finance or accounting coursework and some development jobs that require construction management or engineering skills.

LICENSING

Most states require you to obtain a license before you can sell real estate. The requirements vary from state to state, but in most cases, getting a license entails taking real estate classes, passing an exam, or both. In California, real estate agents are required to take three classes before they can start practicing. To become a broker, you need to take an additional exam. New York requires salespeople to pass an exam in addition to 45 hours of class work; brokers are required to have worked in the field for 2 years, have passed an additional 45 hours of class work, and have passed an additional exam. Some other positions in the industry, such as appraiser, have a credentialing requirement as well. Not to worry; few people have complained about the real estate exam being difficult. Some Californians gripe that the driver's license exam is harder. Additionally, some states hand out exemptions to people who have college-level real estate course work or law degrees. You'll need to check with your home state to find out what the licensing requirements are for your particular region.

Acquisition and Development

SITE ACQUISITION SPECIALIST

Acquisition specialists work with developers or corporate development groups to identify and secure property for development. That is, the acquisition specialist sources new deals. A specialist's role might include market research, discussions with brokers and sales agents to identify properties for sale and market trends, analysis of zoning requirements, and interaction and negotiation with relevant parties to secure a property. The role is an excellent stepping-stone for the job of acquisition manager and other higher-level positions. Oftentimes, the acquisition specialist role will have a sales component where you'll be expected to be able to close deals.

Average acquisition specialist salaries range from $70,000 to $100,000.

FINANCIAL ANALYST

Financial analysts are the right-hand men and women to asset managers, and as such the financial analyst position is a viable stepping-stone to higher-level asset management and acquisition roles. The financial analyst typically spends his or her day meeting with borrowers, lenders, and brokers as well as maintaining and updating asset valuation models for the company's portfolio. You might meet with brokers to see what new properties are coming on the market or what direction the market is going in terms of occupancy levels and prospective tenants. You'd then update your financial models to reflect this information. So, unlike many financial analyst roles, this one is "high touch" in that it requires near constant interaction with people in the industry. Indeed, much of the role is taking intangible information—the gut feels and opinions of brokers, lenders, and clients—and quantifying it as part of your model.

Average financial analyst salaries on the acquisition side range from $40,000 to $85,000.

LAND DEVELOPMENT/HOMEBUILDER PROJECT MANAGER

Project managers oversee the full life cycle of the development process from site selection to construction. A project manager might perform due diligence with respect to land acquisitions, negotiate with government agencies, secure the proper permits for development, prepare and manage project budgets, and manage contractors through the construction process. Project managers often arrive at their positions after working in construction management or architecture.

Salaries for the position range from $70,000 to $125,000 depending on the market.

REIT/INVESTMENT FUND ASSET MANAGER

Asset fund managers oversee a portfolio of real estate investments. Typical duties include selection of properties to acquire or dispose of, oversight of the due diligence process, negotiation with buyers and sellers, and oversight of properties while they are in a portfolio to ensure that they are meeting performance goals. Fund managers typically have significant real estate experience in addition to a graduate professional degree such as an MBA or JD.

Salaries are typically well in excess of $150,000. Funds often offer managers incentives based on fund performance that significantly increase a manager's earning potential.

Brokerage and Sales

RESIDENTIAL SALES AGENT

Real estate agents represent buyers and sellers in the home-selling process. Buyer agents facilitate the transaction for buyers by helping them find homes and negotiate prices and for sellers by helping them market their homes. Agents from the same firm rarely represent both buyers and sellers in the same transaction.

Agents need to be versed in local demographics and market climate, real estate law, financing, government programs, and housing law. Agents must be licensed by their state to practice. Requirements vary but usually consist of an education program and examination. Licenses allow agents to practice only in the state and specific residential market in which they are licensed, and they must practice under a broker. Other than a relatively straightforward licensing process, there are few barriers to becoming a residential agent. Many of the most successful agents have no more than a high school diploma, but have an abundance of market savvy.

Typically, buyer and seller agents evenly split a commission that averages 6 percent of the home sale price. Agents split their fee with their broker, the split being on a sliding scale. New agents split fees evenly with brokers, while an experienced agent may take in 80 percent of the commission. Independent offices like RE/MAX allow agents to take in nearly 100 percent of their commission.

Salaries for agents vary greatly by market and by the aggressiveness of the salesperson.

RESIDENTIAL BROKER

Like residential agents, brokers bring together buyers and sellers in real estate transactions. The primary distinction between sales agents and brokers is one of licensing. Brokers have typically undergone a more rigorous licensing process that requires greater work experience, training, and examination than that of the agent. Unlike agents, brokers can practice real estate independently. If you want to go into business for yourself, you'll need to become a broker.

Salaries for residential brokers also vary greatly by market and by the aggressiveness of the salesperson, though the range sits at the higher end of what residential agents earn.

 INSIDER TIP

Because brokers rely heavily or solely on commission-based compensation, the ramp-up period for a commercial broker can be lean.

COMMERCIAL BROKER

Commercial brokers, too, bring together buyers and sellers in real estate transactions. Unlike residential brokers, corporate brokers tend to specialize in the representation of buyers or tenants, sellers, or builders in the office, retail, or industrial sectors. Brokerage on the buyer or seller representative side tends to be more lucrative than that of the building representative side. Commercial brokers tend to be well versed in the market dynamics, business climate, and demographics of a geographic market. Their expertise and value lie in their ability to understand a market as well as client needs.

Sales cycles are extremely long in commercial brokerage; it may take a year or more from the time a broker begins a relationship with a client until he or she executes a transaction. Because brokers rely heavily or solely on commission-based compensation, the ramp-up period for a commercial broker can be lean. Tenant and landlord brokers typically split a commission that averages approximately 5 percent of the lease value; the tenant representative will take 3 percent, the landlord representative 2 percent. Brokers might receive 50 percent of their commission at signing, with the remainder paid out as the lease progresses. Broker compensation starts low but climbs as the client base grows. A new broker may only earn $30,000 to $40,000 in the first year, but up to $50,000 to $100,000 in the third or fourth year. Once a broker has ramped up, he or she can earn well in excess of $150,000. A commercial broker's income can reach dizzying heights. As one insider says, "The sky's the limit after 5 to 10 years."

Some investment real estate firms view commercial brokerage, coupled with an MBA, as a good training ground for the investment real estate business. Commercial brokerage jobs are often difficult to attain. Most brokers enter the business through industry contacts. Midcareer job switchers often enter brokerage with significant sales experience in other industries. Undergraduates can explore commercial brokerage through internships offered at some firms. Industry insiders see marketing associate, marketing manager, and other allied market-facing roles in commercial brokerage as a viable and proven route to a commercial broker position.

MARKETING ASSOCIATE, COMMERCIAL BROKERAGE

Marketing associates support commercial brokers in the areas of tenant, building, or owner representation. Their primary duties are to develop the general market requirements for their region as well as the specific requirements for tenants, buildings, or owners in their area. Marketing associates have the opportunity to move to a broker role as they progress in their careers.

Salaries range from $30,000 to $60,000 depending on experience and location.

Property Management

PROPERTY MANAGER

Property managers manage and lease properties for owners. Their day-to-day duties include a broad spectrum of activities including leasing or managing the leasing out of property to tenants, handling tenant complaints and relations, maintaining building occupancy levels, maintaining desired lease rates, preparing reports for property owners, preparing budgets, hiring service employees, collecting rents, paying bills, negotiating contracts, and maintaining and repairing property. Additionally, they'll run reports on the group of properties they manage to make sure that they're bringing in enough income and that their expenses are in line. Property managers, sometimes called portfolio managers, may also need a real estate sales or broker license, as they are often called on to do leasing, especially at junior levels.

Property managers often arrive at their positions through previous work as a leasing agent tenant services representative, assistant property manager, or other specialist within the property management field.

Average property manager salaries range from $60,000 to $100,000, depending on geography. Entry-level assistant property manager salaries range from $30,000 to $50,000.

LEASING AGENT

Leasing agents carry out the sales role at property management firms, receiving a commission or flat fee for finding, qualifying, and closing sales. Often, leasing agents require sales or broker licenses.

Average leasing agent salaries range from $45,000 to $65,000, depending on commission structure.

Finance

LOAN OFFICER

Loan officers work for mortgage banks, qualifying borrowers for mortgages and preparing loan terms. Depending on the institution, a loan officer might be required to find his or her own leads. Loan officers usually receive a commission of approximately $1,500 per loan processed for a typical loan.

Salaries for loan officers can average $85,000 to $115,000 on up, depending on the market in which the officer operates.

MORTGAGE BROKER

Mortgage brokers are salespeople who bring together borrowers and lenders. A mortgage broker will typically receive a client from a real estate agent or broker. He or she will determine the best loan for the client and negotiate the terms of the loan for the client.

Mortgage brokers typically receive commissions between 1 and 5 percent of loan amounts and can earn more than $80,000 per year.

FINANCIAL ANALYST/LEASING ANALYST

Financial and credit analysts provide a wide spectrum of functions in the real estate finance sector. Functions include analysis of mortgage loans for developers, analysis of potential loans to make sure they meet lending qualifications, or preparation of loans for pooling. Analyst roles at major financial institutions are considered a training ground for further work in REITs and development companies.

Base salaries for these roles, which require a bachelor's degree and a strong finance or mathematics background, range from $45,000 to $65,000.

Ancillary Services

ESCROW COORDINATOR/CLOSING AGENT

The closing agent's role is first and foremost one of coordination. The agent ensures that buyers and sellers have signed and properly filled out the staggering array of forms necessary to close on a piece of property.

Salaries range from $30,000 to $50,000.

APPRAISER

Real estate appraisers estimate the value of properties for taxation or valuation purposes using a series of standard methodologies. Though they are relatively immune to the cycles of the industry, appraisal positions are somewhat insular within the industry and don't offer the mobility across functions as do other positions.

Typical appraiser salaries range from $45,000 to $80,000.

TITLE OFFICER

Title officers search public records to determine whether the property being sold is actually owned by the seller, has a lien against it, or is otherwise influenced in such a way that will affect the parties undergoing the transaction.

Salaries typically range from $30,000 to $50,000.

Corporate Real Estate

REAL ESTATE DEVELOPMENT MANAGER

The development manager drives the selection and development process for new corporate real estate sites. Managers serve as subject matter experts for corporate decision makers, plan and execute the development of new sites, and develop long-term solutions for a corporation's real estate needs. During the development process, the manager will negotiate with brokers and maintain oversight of the build-out process. After moving into a new space, a development manager will typically also oversee relationships with property managers. The development manager translates the strategic needs of the company into real estate terms. As such, he or she is often involved in high-level or long-term planning sessions in fast-growing companies.

Average salaries for development managers range from $75,000 to $150,000.

Real People Profiles

DIRECTOR OF ASSET MANAGEMENT, PRIVATE REAL ESTATE FUND

Age: 32
Years in role: 6
Education: MBA
Background: 3 years as development project manager, residential developer
Annual salary: more than $200,000 (how far over depends on fund/REIT performance)

The Work

Asset management funds tend to be lean organizations. "We have 20 people in our firm, a senior partner, three managing directors, myself, and 15 support people," says an insider. A director of asset management typically has three major job functions: managing assets, looking out for new deals, and handling sales and purchases.

Managing assets occupies most of an asset manager's time between deals. He must ensure occupancy is high on portfolio properties, rents are high, and capital expenditures are within budget while securing and negotiating small-scale financing for capital improvements.

Asset managers constantly look for new properties to add to the portfolio. To do this, the asset manager keeps a close eye on the markets in which his fund operates. He talks to brokers frequently to discover which properties will become available and what the occupancy and rent trends are, and to get a sense of the overall business climate. With an understanding of what properties may be coming on the market and what the occupancy and rent outlooks portend, he develops models for various properties. If the management team decides to pursue a space, he and a partner will lead negotiations to complete the deal.

Finally, the asset manager works on sales and financing. This entails selling properties that are ready to be disposed of and seeking capital from potential fund investors.

"Unlike venture capital funds, real estate funds both underwrite funds and manage the business. We dread visits from ourselves," says one insider, who adds, "It's a rewarding business. To be successful, you need to exercise a broad range of skills: quantitative skills to model and evaluate scenarios; people skills to negotiate with everyone from leaseholders to third-party providers and purchasing agents; and marketing and sales skills to sell buildings, get people into buildings, and sell the fund."

However, landing a position at an asset management firm can be tough. Says an insider, "Firms don't recruit at many MBA programs. For the most part, you have to scrape and be creative." Being creative and scraping means networking through every possible venue. Additionally, a strong finance background is critical. An insider adds that it is helpful to get as much industry experience as possible from either "the supply or demand side"—that is, from development project management or commercial brokerage respectively.

A Day in the Life

7:30   Arrive at the office, check e-mail. The in-box is choked with an e-mail thread from business school friends.

8:00   Call local leasing brokers. Get update on leases.

9:00   Spend the rest of the morning calling on property management companies in the fund's nonlocal markets. My company has the critical mass to manage local properties by itself. Get status on budget items and minor capital improvements from property managers.

12:00   Usually head out to the gym during lunch. Today, the weather is beautiful. It's always beautiful in Southern California, so instead I run 3 miles through downtown and finish with a few flights up the convention center stairs.

1:00   Call brokers to negotiate a lease.

2:00   Make some calls to local brokers to assess potential of some new assets in our market. Three properties look good.

3:00   Call our attorney to check status of lease, purchase agreement, and loans.

3:30   Surf the Net until management meeting.

4:00   Management team meeting. Evaluate new properties based on our strategy in local market. Discuss whether we need to fine-tune strategy.

5:00   Finish modeling IRR potential of short-listed assets.

6:30   Head home to see my wife and new baby.

COMMERCIAL REAL ESTATE BROKER, TENANT REPRESENTATIVE

Age: 33
Years in role: 3
Education: college
Background: 4 years in industrial sales, military
Annual salary: $90,000 (bad year) to $130,000 (good year)

The Work

Tenant representative commercial brokers work to find the right space for their tenant clients. To do this, they build relationships with their clients to understand their ongoing real estate needs, absorb and keep abreast of a geographic market's demographic characteristics, and maintain the ability to perform analyses necessary to evaluate the financial merits of a property. "Being a commercial real estate broker is like having your own consulting firm," says an insider.

Success as a broker rests on the broker's ability to build long-term client relationships and to understand client needs. Because of this, it often takes a substantial amount of time—up to 10 years—to reach steady state as a broker. "Really, you're working for yourself rather than a brokerage firm," says an insider at a boutique brokerage firm. A typical sales cycle includes acquiring clients, often through cold calls; researching the market, client needs, and available spaces to find a suitable fit for the client; and finally negotiating deal points and seeing those points through completion of a contract.

Commercial brokerage demands endurance. Unlike residential real estate brokerage, the commercial brokerage sales cycle can extend to more than 2 years. A broker may handle anywhere from ten to 15 clients simultaneously, requiring no small project management skills on the part of the broker. Many firms offer only commission-based compensation, but seasoned brokers like it that way; straight commission allows them to cut a bigger piece of the deal pie for themselves. Finally, like the entire real estate industry, brokers are subject to the hyperbolic swings of the business cycle. "You've really got to have a stomach for the downturns," says an insider.

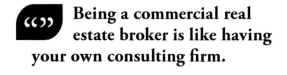 **Being a commercial real estate broker is like having your own consulting firm.**

A Day in the Life

7:00   Check e-mail from home.

8:30   Meet with a client's real estate team, one of the few growing software companies in San Francisco, for a walk through a larger space—that of a recently departed dot com.

11:00   Cold calls—call contacts from the list I composed of both recent social contacts and companies I researched in the San Francisco Business Journal.

12:30   Lunch with Big Five consulting firm client at Palomino. It's a social lunch, and I get to take a pulse of the firm's needs.

1:30   Meet with landlord and tenant lawyers to negotiate lease. My role is to make sure that the deal points get into the lease.

3:00   Set up appointments for the following day.

4:00   Walk through another space with law firm client. Yet again, we're looking at a former dot-com space.

6:00   Review points of lease we negotiated today, check e-mail, review prospect list for tomorrow's cold calls.

7:00   Take a quick trip to the gym and hope to get home by 8:00 to make dinner with my fiancée.

RESIDENTIAL REAL ESTATE AGENT

Age: 37
Years in role: 5
Education: college
Background: arts administration, artist
Annual salary: $60,0000

The Work

Residential brokerage is sales, pure and simple. Whether you're representing sellers or buyers, you're getting people to commit to a purchase. The job consists primarily of getting sellers to list their property with you as well as convincing buyers to have you represent them. Among the administrative aspects of the job is getting clients to do the paperwork to close a deal. What makes an agent particularly effective, aside from the usual sales skills, is having a thorough understanding of the local market—the recent sales prices, tax rates, quality of schools, and traffic patterns as well as an understanding of where the market and region are headed.

With all the noise out there, getting your name known is extremely important. In the suburbs, people do things like put their faces on shopping carts and go door to door—that's harder to do in New York City, where there are few shopping carts and people would call the cops if you were to bang on their door. The concept is the same, though. You make yourself known in social circles and imprint on them your name as one that stands for trust and market savvy. It helps having some sort of affiliation with your target market—as an artist, for instance, you can better understand the needs of that community—that's how you have to market yourself, at least. Then you have to sell. This might mean something like going to parties and giving people an idea of what homes are selling for in their neighborhood—get them juiced up a bit and then get them to get you to list their apartment or condo.

Not everyone will want to work with you, but selling is a numbers game. You have to contact as many people as you can—make lists of people to contact on a given day and follow through. Sure, people will be abrupt. It's definitely not a business for the thin-skinned. The other thing to realize is that you're always "on" in the profession. Your cell phone is always on, and you take calls whenever they come in. And when you consider that people are going to call you after working hours, it means that your weekends and evenings are devoted to your profession.

A Day in the Life

7:00   Go to the gym—there's no time in the evening.

8:30   Read the paper. Drink coffee.

9:00   Have an appointment with the stager—stagers are those pixies that clear apartments of heavy furniture and the smell of chicken fat and fill it with rented furniture, fresh paint, and flowers to accentuate a home's potential. I convinced the seller that getting a stager to do a quick painting of the wall and cleaning up of the apartment (staging it) would goose the sales price of the house significantly. I talk with the stager to see what kind of rental furniture she plans on bringing in.

10:00   Coffee (again) with potential buyer I met through a mutual friend. It's a friendly chat, but I assess his needs and get him to feel that I'm an expert in the market.

10:30   Call another seller to arrange for an inspector to come later in the week.

11:00   I arrange for a few hours of time to work on my own art project—there's usually a lull during the middle of the day, so I take a few hours out to work in the studio.

2:30   It starts back up—I spend the rest of the afternoon fielding calls and e-mails from my listings.

6:00   I arrange to show a buyer a two-bedroom on the Upper West Side and a one-bedroom in the same neighborhood.

7:00   I show a different buyer a condo in Chelsea—luckily I'm still on the West Side.

7:30   I take that same buyer down to another, smaller place in the West Village.

8:00   Done for the day.

The Workplace

Lifestyle, Hours, and Culture

Diversity

Compensation

Benefits

Career Path

Insider Scoop

Lifestyle, Hours, and Culture

Lifestyle and culture vary greatly throughout the industry, but relationship building and entrepreneurship tint most sectors of real estate. With the absence of truly large corporate structures, people in real estate tend to be more entrepreneurial than those who work in traditional corporate environments. Brokers think of themselves as independent consultants within their offices; asset fund directors actively manage operations of their investments. Much of the compensation structure throughout the industry is performance based, so if you are the type that needs to be jump-started, real estate probably isn't for you. Additionally, relationship building is critical for getting referrals, generating leads, and keeping abreast of subtle changes in the marketplace. "Commercial brokers know more about what's going on at most companies in an area than the employees themselves," says an insider. People in real estate see just about any social network as a way to build relationships; of course, there is the old saw about doing business on the golf course, but people in the industry find other ways to network, including through religious groups and charitable organizations.

Relationship building tends to bind real estate professionals to geographic markets. It takes time and effort to build strong networks and develop a good understanding of your local territory; people aren't willing to give that up. "If I moved to another market, I'd have to start over," says one insider.

Business relationships tend to spill over into personal relationships. Brokers and sales people often conduct business over golf or other recreational events. "If I take a broker out to a game or for a round of golf, is that work or is that pleasure? It's hard to distinguish the two in this industry," says one insider. "These are the people I call if I need tickets to the Red Sox game," says another. People in the industry tend to be social creatures and are happy with this arrangement. "These are people I've known for the past 5 years. We've evolved together," one broker says of his clients.

Real estate professionals tend to work long, but flexible hours. Much of the work is selling, which happens all the time. An insider says, "No one tells you to work long hours, but if you want to build up a good practice for yourself, it's understood that's what you do." For the real estate investment community, workload comes in thunderstorm-like spurts. "It's pretty routine here managing assets that we have in our portfolio, but when we buy or sell an asset, all hell breaks loose," says an insider. Seventy-plus hour weeks aren't uncommon when a deal is in the works. At other times, the week is closer to a more manageable 50 hours. For brokers, the line between leisure and work blurs even more. "The cell phone is always on, and I'll answer client calls at 11:00 at night or on the weekend," says an insider. You have to work on your client's schedule, and for the most part, since they have a job outside of real estate, you have to meet them on their terms, which are often evenings and weekends. Retail brokers average 50-hour weeks, though the distribution of hours can vary greatly depending on the number of closings you have.

Commercial brokers know more about what's going on at most companies in an area than the employees themselves.

Diversity

The state of diversity in the real estate industry varies greatly from sector to sector. Residential real estate brokerage firms tend to look a lot like the communities they serve. Commercial brokerages were, until very recently, male-dominated clubs. This, however, has begun to change. Diversity has not flowered in boutique institutional investment firms and development firms as much as in other areas largely because of the way companies fill positions—word of mouth and personal networks. The institutional real estate finance world has made greater strides in promoting diversity as it relies on the same diversity practices that govern the broader financial institutions of which they are a part. That is, the more "corporate" the job, the more likely there will be formal diversity-recruiting programs in place. Fannie Mae ranks high on a number of lists as a good place to work for minorities and women. Organizations such as Freddie Mac, Fannie Mae, and the Mortgage Bankers Association of America have created programs to promote diversity in the real estate finance sector.

Compensation

Without equivocation, many real estate professionals will tell you that they are in it for the money. Still, different functional areas offer vastly different compensation opportunities. Most people in the industry spend a few years in lower-paying positions before their earnings begin to take off. As an undergraduate entering the market, you might earn anywhere from $25,000 to $45,000, with the exception of financial analyst positions, which earn more. As an MBA, you'll earn less than your colleagues who chose more traditional postgraduate careers. Average MBA salaries from top-20 schools start around $70,000 for most real estate positions. However, if you exit your MBA program with substantial industry experience, you'll earn significantly more than your colleagues who are switching careers.

Experienced commercial brokers and asset managers have the potential to earn well in excess of $150,000 annually, pushed into orbit by performance-based compensation. Retail broker and agent income can reach stratospheric heights as well, but tend to be less common and lower than that of commercial brokers. Compensation in property management is more stable with less upside potential. Property managers and affiliated positions often earn a solid base salary, averaging more than $50,000, but without the upside potential of brokerage and investment roles. Roles in the services area also pay a base salary with few performance-based incentives. These roles also have the disadvantage of not being widely transferable across the industry. Corporate real estate positions offer strong base salaries and the incentive programs of the corporations in which they reside.

RESIDENTIAL BROKERAGE COMMISSIONS

Income for residential real estate agents varies dramatically depending on the local housing market, economic climate, and an agent's ability to sell. Agents typically receive no base salary, but a commission consisting of 1 to 3 percent of a home's sale price, established by the agent's agreement with his broker and the type of brokerage for which he works. An independent office model firm such as RE/MAX takes an insignificant cut of commission, leaving the agent with a commission of up to 3 percent of a home's selling price. Traditional brokerage franchises like Coldwell Banker that offer full support for their agents take 20 to 50 percent of an agent's commission based on the agent's experience, leaving the agent with a commission of 1.5 to 2.4 percent of the home's selling price.

To put this in perspective, suppose you're selling in the relatively posh area of Palo Alto, California, and the home's price is $1,120,000. An independent agent could earn nearly 3 percent, or $33,600 on a single sale; a new agent working at a traditional brokerage firm could make around $16,800. Then again, if you're selling in Most Places, U.S.A., you're more likely looking at a commission on $189,000 (the average median home price in January 2005), which would be $5,670 if you're an independent and half that if you're working for a brokerage firm.

COMMERCIAL BROKERAGE COMMISSIONS

Commercial brokers cultivate long-term client relationships in hopes of signing a big deal. Corporations and businesses do not relocate often, but when they do, it can be fruitful for the broker. Tenant and landlord brokers typically split a 5 percent commission, with 60 percent going to the tenant representative and 40 percent to the landlord representative. Market competition can drive this down substantially. Brokers typically receive 50 percent of their commission at signing and the remainder as an income stream that is paid out as a lease commences.

Let's go through an example to get a feel for how much a broker might earn on a single deal: A 100-person professional firm requires approximately 22,000 square feet of office space. Manhattan office space might lease for $30 per square foot. This would make for a lease worth $660,000 per year, or $3,300,000 for a 5-year lease. A tenant representative might then receive approximately $100,000 for closing the deal, $50,000 of which she would get at signing. Commercial brokers typically handle ten to 15 clients at any one time and often work with a client for a year or more before executing a deal.

Benefits

The type of benefits you are likely to receive in the real estate industry depend largely on the sector in which you work, and can be divided between brokerage firms and the rest of the industry. Brokerage firms typically offer their agents paltry benefits packages and often do not contribute to health-care premiums. When you move away from brokerage firms to companies that have a greater proportion of non-commission–based employees, benefits packages become more substantial. Trammell Crow, which offers a host of real estate services in addition to brokerage, boasts a suite of benefits including health care and 401(k). Corporate real estate team members and financial services professionals generally receive benefits packages on par with the respective corporations and financial services firms. Large financial services companies with real estate groups such as Prudential Financial Services offer the best benefits packages, with wide plan choices and employer contributions to retirement plans.

Travel in the real estate industry is generally minimal. Because of the intensely local nature of the industry, professionals have a limited realm in which they can be effective. The exception to this is the resort or vacation properties sector, where properties tend to be managed remotely. In this case, professionals travel often. "You can't passively manage a real estate asset and be successful; this means plenty of travel," says an insider.

Vacation time, like benefits, tends not to follow the pattern of corporate America. Real estate professionals tend to work when there is work to be done. "I can't afford to miss out on a sales opportunity," says one insider.

Career Path

The real estate industry has few major tracks, which rarely converge with one another. Careers in residential brokerage and the rest of the industry rarely meet. If you enter the profession as a residential agent, you'll likely stay in residential brokerage. Property management professionals sometimes cross into brokerage or investment roles, but generally stay within the property management arena. Some of the paths leading to property manager include leasing agent and assistant property manager. People in ancillary service roles also tend to remain in their fields. Corporate real estate management executives are often considered strategic or development personnel and are culled from the ranks of commercial brokerage and real estate investment. Commercial brokerage and real estate investment positions tend to have the most currency and exchange value in the industry.

Commercial brokerage offers opportunities not only to advance as a broker, but also to move into real estate investment and asset management. Commercial brokerage is often difficult to enter, requiring relationships with people in the industry. Paths include sales positions in other industries, college internships, and marketing associate and manager positions within commercial brokerages. Commercial brokers often tap marketing managers and specialists for coveted broker roles. As support personnel for brokers, they know better than most people what the market requirements are and often make a good fit for the brokerage role from both the perspectives of background and personality.

Real estate investment and asset management positions are among the most coveted in the industry. Top positions as partners in asset management or development firms are few, and competition for them is fierce. Both the commercial brokerage and development and construction sectors are popular training grounds for this work. Combined with an MBA and a Rolodex full of contacts, these positions offer the best chance at breaking into real estate investment management. Finance roles offer some inroads into investment management, but aren't as firmly established stepping-stones as they are in other industries. Unlike venture capital or investment banking, real estate asset managers actively manage the operational aspects of their investments, and therefore operating experience in a critical area like brokerage or development is unparalleled.

Insider Scoop

WHAT EMPLOYEES REALLY LIKE

Thrill of the Deal

Most high-profile real estate positions require great deal-making expertise and can involve monumental architecture. Putting the deal together requires a wide range of soft and hard skills, and insiders say they relish the thrill of the big deal.

Money, Money, Money

Real estate can be very lucrative. For commercial brokers, some retail brokers, mortgage brokers, fund managers, and others who garner percentages of transactions, real estate offers nearly limitless financial rewards.

People Who Need People

Real estate is no industry for wallflowers. "Real estate is by all measures a people business," says an insider. Industry professionals work in the same markets for many years and cultivate deep relationships that transcend business.

Uncorporate Culture

The industry is laden with independent business people and bound together by relationships that tie people together between companies rather than just within them.

This fosters a culture that the freewheeling spirits of real estate heartily endorse: Professionals work flexible hours and conduct business in pleasurable environments like the golf course or over dinner.

Building the Future

Real estate, and especially development, gives you the opportunity to put a mark on the world and leave a legacy. On a grand scale, Donald Trump's buildings that litter Manhattan's skyline bear this out. As does Arthur Levitt's Levittown. On a smaller scale, one insider we talked to said there was something very cool about naming a street in a subdivision after himself: "Go on Yahoo! Maps, type in my name, comma, Tucson Arizona." Sure enough, Yahoo pinpointed the street bearing his name.

The Real in Real Estate

Insiders like the fact that they deal with tangible products. They get satisfaction in being able to walk into the thing they've built, financed, sold, or project managed.

WATCH OUT!

Feast or Famine

The business is relentlessly cyclical. Good times are great, but are inevitably followed by long, deep troughs. For the ilk of sales people that rely solely on commission for income, holding out through lean years requires an iron will. The ability to deal with uncertainty is a personal quality that will make life easier if you go into this field.

Geography is Destiny

Real estate requires an intimate knowledge of idiosyncratic geographic markets that takes many years to master; even Donald Trump only operates in Manhattan and Atlantic City. "You cannot switch markets without starting over to some degree," says one insider. If you like being tied down to a single community, real estate should work for you; if you've got wanderlust, beware.

The Old Boys Network

Real estate is still an industry where connections go a long way in breaking in, making deals, and getting funding. There's room for those outside the traditional old boys network, but you're likely to run into some archaic attitudes in this industry, too. And make sure that you brush up on those networking skills.

Testing the Virtue of Patience

Real estate projects rival Russian novels in length. Commercial brokers might spend years cultivating a relationship with a client before ever, if at all, fulfilling a deal with them. Real estate investment firms often hold portfolio properties at least 3 to 5 years. Building a track record or establishing a practice entails having the endurance to see a multitude of deals through to fruition.

The Hours

Industry insiders carp about the hours they keep, though the complaints vary depending on sector. Asset managers note that their work becomes extremely hectic when they purchase or dispose of a new property. Commercial brokers say that they keep long hours, with 12-hour days being commonplace, when they are building their practices. Mortgage brokers and residential brokers say that they are "always on."

Paving Over Paradise

Though the more eco-friendly developments have taken hold, those who are squeamish about putting a strip mall on a newt breeding ground, for example, might work in conflict with their ideals. Put more bluntly, one insider says, "Most developers aren't into sustainable development; if it doesn't help the bottom line, we won't do it."

Getting Hired

Requirements

Real estate agents and brokers must have a deep understanding of local tax laws, zoning regulations, school districts, contracts, building repair, utilities, transportation, business, architectural styles, and much more. They must know how to use computers. The Internet in particular is a growing part of the real estate trade. People are increasingly using it to buy and sell houses, and a real estate professional who is not Web-savvy will be left in the dust.

LICENSING

Agents and Brokers

All 50 states require real estate agents and brokers to be licensed. To get a license, a prospective agent must be 18 years old, hold a high school diploma, and pass a written test. Most states also require prospective agents to complete courses in real estate. Brokers need between 60 and 90 hours of class time plus 1 to 3 years of experience selling real estate as an agent or a bachelor's degree in real estate. As transactions become more complex, more firms are looking to hire college graduates. Classes in real estate, business, statistics, and economics will give you a competitive edge.

Appraisers

All 50 states require appraisers to be licensed. There are national organizations that offer real estate appraisers professional certification in residential appraising, commercial appraising, and agricultural appraising. Appraisers often start their real estate careers as real estate agents, where they acquire vital knowledge about the market. However, it's increasingly common for college graduates with course work in business, economics, finance, architecture, law, or engineering to enter the appraisal profession directly as appraisal assistants.

OTHER REQUIREMENTS

Property managers often go further if they hold a college degree in business, accounting, finance, or real estate. Many property managers enter the industry as real estate agents, a career that offers helpful experience in showing properties and in understanding the ins and outs of the industry's laws and regulations. Those who wish to pursue careers as asset managers should take courses in finance, taxes, and real estate in general.

Developers should have a strong understanding of business in general and the real estate industry in particular. A college degree with course work in architecture, labor management, business, law, economics, and engineering is helpful, if not necessary. Most developers have previous real estate experience, but they can also enter the field as assistants working for development firms.

The Recruiting Process

With a few exceptions, the real estate industry doesn't have a formal college or midcareer recruiting process. Investment banks, life insurance companies, and pension funds recruit a limited number of undergraduates and MBAs for finance roles. A few asset management funds will tap MBAs at select programs. For the most part, though, the industry's reputation for relying on relationships extends to recruiting. "I have to admit, I got into the industry because I was referred to someone in a boutique commercial brokerage," says one insider, who adds, "It's very old school." Investment and development firms operate in highly specialized markets and generally rely on referrals and industry contacts to fill their needs. (For advice on how to network effectively, check out the WetFeet Insider Guide *Networking Works!*)

Nevertheless, persistence and salesmanship can pay. One successful asset manager cold called prospects in asset funds and partnerships. Though he had, at best, limited connections with the firms, he received a number of interviews and eventually landed a job at an asset management partnership.

Of course, networking is a necessary, but not sufficient, condition for landing a job. "There are high barriers to entry in this field," says an insider in an institutional investment firm. REITs and asset management funds look for specific experience in their associates—usually backgrounds in commercial brokerage or construction management and development, with an MBA in finance or real estate. One insider landed a job in corporate real estate based on his background as an architect and construction manager. Larger financial management firms look for entry-level candidates with undergraduate degrees in finance, accounting, or analytical majors like mathematics. Commercial brokerages often look for people who are accomplished in commission-based sales.

Residential brokerage has the lowest education and experience barriers of the major real estate tracks. Residential agents aren't generally required to have completed any higher education before entering the field and often join the ranks through word of mouth.

Interviewing Tips

Interviewing tips for the real estate industry vary as much as the diverse functions within the industry. For the most part, with the exception of jobs in corporate real estate and financial institutions, the industry doesn't have a formal recruiting process. This translates into an equally informal interviewing process.

Almost all real estate companies look for three things in a potential hire:

- People skills

- An entrepreneurial bent

- A constitution that can withstand bad times

The real estate industry values experience and the ability to execute, and to prove candidates worthy, some companies have been known to take the case interview to extremes. One insider says of his experience interviewing with an asset management partnership, "We spoke on the phone, and the interview was this: Fly up to Calgary on Monday. Look at an office property we're thinking of acquiring there. Talk to the property manager, brokers, and whomever you see fit. Tell us what you think on Wednesday." At your interview, being prepared to handle this level of stress successfully and with a positive attitude will make it that much more likely a firm will welcome you as part of its team. Be prepared for less grandiose interviews, but with the same test of mettle—remember, companies are looking for someone who can sniff out deals, make contacts, gather market intelligence through talking to people, and sell, sell, sell.

Appearances are as important as anything else in the industry. If you get a call back from a recruiter or hiring manager, be sure to call her back promptly—treat the situation as a sales opportunity. You may want to consider being more aggressive about landing an interview. Though this can be a risky maneuver, you could initiate a call to a firm you believe might be hiring—you are embodying the behavior that firms are looking for—taking initiative, being aggressive, sniffing out opportunities, showing off your interpersonal skills, and getting your prospective employer interested in your appeal within 15 to 30 seconds. If they see your moxie, you've gone a long way toward distinguishing yourself from the thundering herd.

Getting Grilled

Real estate investment managers and sales people make enormous business decisions based on limited data. The emphasis for them is on decision, rather than data. This is not to say they won't assess your analytical skills (for investment management and financial analyst positions, at least). It's just that soft skills play a major role in the industry. Expect questions that'll give your interviewer insight into how your decision process works and that you can make decisions. Also expect questions that will force you to give your opinion on a subject. Finally, be sure to close the interview properly—with a question that requires some follow up or action on the part of the interviewer. Typical closing questions include, "So what is the next step in the process?" or "When can I expect to hear from you?" Here are some of the types of questions you might encounter:

GENERAL AND SALES QUESTIONS

- Tell me about the last job that you worked in a sales role.

- How many calls do you expect to make a day?

- Tell me about your experience working in a team and what your role typically was.

- Tell me about how you handle stress.

- Why would you be good for a career in real estate?

- What was your typical role on sales teams you've been on? What role do you like to be in?

- How do your coworkers describe you?

- What are the things a buyer wants to know about a house?

- How do you handle buyer objections?

- How do you qualify potential buyers?

- What are some of the prospecting techniques you use?

ASSET ACQUISITION AND MANAGEMENT QUESTIONS

- Why do you want to work in our firm? What interests you about our specialization?

- Why should we hire you? (If you're talking to a partner at a major real estate investment firm who brings in millions of dollars a year, this can be daunting. Remember, confidence—but not cockiness—is a big plus in the industry.)

- How will you source properties? (Remember, if you are on the acquisition side, you'll be expected to bring in potential properties. You do this by using your established network and building a broader network all the while.)

- Where do you think the real estate market is headed? (Remember that the market zigs and zags differently for each sector and geography—be specific why you think the office market in San Diego will retain value—know the vacancy rates, average rent, what local companies are doing and how demand will change in the short and long term, what other players in the industry are doing and what supply looks like in the short and long term.)

- What property would you invest in now? (That'll be your job, after all.)

Grilling your Interviewer

The following interview questions will fit many real estate interview situations. Of course, you'll want to come up with questions specific to the role for which you are interviewing as well as to the company with which you're interviewing and the market at hand. We've grouped questions according to risk. The rare are softballs that'll be easy for your interviewer to field. Of course, the risk with rare questions is that your interviewer might get bored. Well-done questions are curve balls and sliders that will have your interviewer on her toes. You might want to try throwing out some rare questions in order to get a feel for your interviewer before going to the tough questions.

RARE

- What do you like best about your job, and what do you dislike?

- What are some of the best deals you have done?

- How does your team work?

- What's the best property you ever acquired?

MEDIUM

- What are the advantages of your company over other ones in the industry?

- Where do you see the market going?

- How is your company protected against an industry downturn?

- How have you shifted your strategy to accommodate changes in the industry?

- Which competitor do you fear most?

- How are deals currently sourced at your company?

- What kind of support can you offer me (marketing, sales, advertising, etc.)?

WELL DONE

- What is the worst deal you've ever done, and what could have been done to improve it?

- Will I get a closer of my own?

- What will my percentage of fund profits be?

For Your Reference

Industry Glossary

Recommended Reading

Industry Associations

Additional Resources

Industry Glossary

Adjustable-rate mortgage (ARM). A mortgage that lets the lender adjust the interest rate at specified intervals to match current interest rates.

Adjusted basis. The cost of a property as well as any capital improvements, less depreciation.

Amortization term. The time required to fully amortize a loan, usually expressed in months. A 30-year mortgage has a term of 360 months. A 15-year mortgage has a term of 180 months.

Annual percentage rate (APR). The cost of a mortgage including interest rate, mortgage insurance, and points.

Assumable mortgage. A mortgage that can be transferred between owners when a house is sold.

Balloon mortgage. A mortgage whose term is fixed, at 360 months for instance, but whose payment size increases over time. Final payments are often in the form of a lump sum. The payment scheme is geared toward buyers who anticipate increased earning potential later in their careers.

Capitalization rate. The capitalization rate, or cap rate, is a measure for valuing properties. You can determine cap rate by dividing a property's annual net (minus taxes, maintenance, etc.) rental income by its anticipated sales price and multiplying by 100. In this way, a cap rate can be used to value the income on an investment relative to other real estate, as well as fixed income, investments.

Closing costs. The costs involved in transferring a property from a seller to a buyer, which include origination costs, attorneys' fees, and title and insurance fees.

Collateralized mortgage obligations (CMOs). A mortgage-backed bond that separates mortgage pools into different maturity classes, thereby reducing the risk associated with the security.

Conventional mortgage. A mortgage not backed by a federal agency such as Fannie Mae or the Veterans Administration.

Convertible ARM. An adjustable-rate mortgage that can be converted to a fixed-rate mortgage under specified conditions.

Deed of trust. In some states a deed of trust serves as a mortgage.

Discount points. Fees charged by lenders that allow homebuyers to secure lower interest rate mortgages. A point is the equivalent of 1 percent of the loan amount. Each point will lower the rate of interest on a mortgage by 0.125 percent. Mortgage bankers will often allow up to 3 discount points.

DownREIT. A variation of an UpREIT, where an REIT operates properties other than those in which it owns a controlling interest.

Equity REIT. A REIT that owns property, as opposed to one that owns mortgages.

Easement. The right to pass through property despite the fact that you don't own the property through which you are passing. Right of way giving persons, other than the owner, who provide access to or over a property.

Escrow. Money deposited with a third party to be delivered upon the fulfillment of a condition. For instance, an escrow agent holds money for taxes and insurance from a homebuyer until a sale is closed.

Fannie Mae. A quasigovernmental agency started in 1968 that originates mortgages for low- and middle-income homebuyers. A loose acronym for the Federal National Mortgage Association.

Financial index. An index is a number to which the interest rate on an adjustable rate mortgage (ARM) is tied. Common indices include LIBOR, the Treasury rate, and CDs.

Finder's fee. A commission paid to a mortgage broker for finding a mortgage loan for a prospective borrower.

Fixed-rate mortgage (FRM). A mortgage in which the interest rate does not change during the entire term of the loan. Fixed-rate mortgages are more common than adjustable-rate mortgages.

Freddie Mac. Like Fannie Mae, a quasi-government company chartered in 1970 to ensure that funds flow to mortgage lenders by buying, securitizing, and investing in home mortgages. A loose acronym for the Federal Home Loan Mortgage Corporation.

Funds from operations (FFO). A measure of REIT operating performance, equal to a REIT's net income including depreciation, excluding gains or losses from sales and acquisitions.

Ginnie Mae. A government-chartered company that buys mortgages from lenders, securitizes them, then markets them to investors, similar to Freddie Mac. A loose acronym for the Government National Mortgage Association (GNMA).

Hybrid REIT. An REIT that owns both mortgages and equities.

Jumbo loan. A loan that exceeds Fannie Mae–approved mortgage limits, usually signifying a big loan for wealthier individuals.

Leverage. The amount of debt in relation to either equity capital or total capital.

LIBOR. The London Interbank Offered Rate. The rate that international banks charge one another for use of funds, similar to the Prime Rate in the United States. LIBOR is an index against which mortgages are based.

Loan origination fee or "points." A fee paid during the processing of a mortgage, expressed as a percentage of a loan. That is, one point equals 1 percent of the total mortgage loan. For example, a $100,000 mortgage with a loan origination fee of 1 point would mean you pay $1,000.

Loan discount points. Fees paid at the beginning of a mortgage that result in a lower interest rate. Each discount point, which equals 1 percent of the total loan amount, will result in a 0.125 percent decrease in the interest rate for a 30-year loan. Discount points are attractive to home owners who intend on staying in their home for a long time.

Mortgage-backed security. A security of bond that is issued by Freddie Mac or a similar organization and is backed by a pool of mortgages.

Multiple listing service (MLS). A group of brokers that share listings (and therefore commissions) in hopes of broadening their audience.

Prime rate. The lending rate that banks charge to other banks. Mortgage rates are often tied to the prime rate.

Real estate investment trust (REIT). REITs are trusts that use pooled funds from investors to buy and manage real estate investments. REITS invest in property (equity REITs), mortgages or similar loans (mortgage REITS), or a combination of the two (hybrid REITs). The vast majority of REITs are of the equity kind. REITs are traded on public exchanges and offer substantially more liquidity than traditional real estate investments, dividend yields of 90 percent of profits, and tax advantages. Additionally, REITs allow small investors to put money in commercial and industrial real estate—something they were previously unable to do.

Real estate operating company (REOC). An REOC is similar to an REIT, but is not required to pay out dividends like an REIT; it also lacks the tax advantages of an REIT. Some companies, such as Starwood Resorts, change structure from REIT to REOC according to their tax situation.

REIT Modernization Act of 1999. Federal tax law change that allows an REIT to own up to 100 percent of stock of a taxable REIT subsidiary that provides services to tenants. The act also lowered the minimum distribution requirement from 95 to 90 percent of an REIT's taxable income.

Title search. A check of the title records to ensure that the seller is the legal owner of the property and that there are no liens against a property.

Underwriting. The process of determining the risk involved for a vendor of a mortgage loan.

UpREIT. In an UpREIT, partners of an REIT and an existing real estate partnership form a new operating partnership. Members of the existing partnership are offered shares of the REIT in exchange for property. This noncash transaction reduces the taxes incurred on the exchange. The advantage of the UpREIT is its tax benefit, which lowers the acquisition cost of new properties for a REIT.

Recommended Reading

Empire: A Tale of Obsession, Betrayal, and the Battle for an American Icon

Mitchell Pacelle (John Wiley and Sons, 2001)

Pacelle's book offers an amazing account of the struggle to control the Empire State building.

The Power Broker: Robert Moses and the Fall of New York

Robert A. Caro (Knopf, 1974)

Master biographer Robert Caro shows how Robert Moses, Parks Commissioner for New York City, became the most influential developer in American history.

Real Estate Finance and Investments (11th ed)

William B. Brueggeman and Jeffrey D. Fisher (McGraw-Hill, 2002)

The definitive book on real estate finance, appropriate for undergraduates and MBAs.

The Real Estate Game: The Intelligent Guide to Decision-Making and Investment

William J. Poorvu and Jeffrey L. Cruikshank (Free Press, 1999)

A Harvard professor's guide to commercial real estate. An excellent primer to the commercial real estate business.

The Millionaire Real Estate Agent

Gary Keller, Dave Jenks, and Jay Papasan (McGraw Hill, 2004)

A bit on the self-help side, this book offers advice on succeeding as an agent and includes case studies from millionaire agents across the United States.

Industry Associations

Global Corporate Real Estate Network (CoreNet)

(www.corenetglobal.org)

Resource for corporate real estate professionals worldwide. CoreNet has more than 3,000 members worldwide.

Institute of Real Estate Management

(www.irem.org)

An affiliate of the National Association of Realtors, IREM is an association focused on the needs of asset managers and property managers.

National Association of Homebuilders

(www.nahb.org)

An organization for the Home Builder community, the NAHB promotes the home-builders' agenda as well as the need to keep a highly skilled workforce in the industry.

National Association of Real Estate Investment Trusts (NAREIT)

(www.nareit.com)

An organization that promotes the interests of REITS and similar organizations. The NAREIT website has many resources for those interested in REIT careers, including industry statistics, a directory of REITS, and a glossary of REIT terms.

National Association of Realtors

(www.realtor.org)

Industry association for retail and commercial real estate agents. It claims to be the world's largest professional association.

Additional Resources

The American Real Estate and Urban Economics Association

(www.areuea.org)

A community of academics, professionals, and policy makers concerned about real estate economics and urban planning issues.

Institutional Real Estate

(www.irei.com)

The self-proclaimed "Gateway to the $4.8 trillion institutional real estate market."

The Journal of Real Estate Finance and Economics

(www.jrefe.org)

An academic journal put out by the University of Georgia.

Knowledge@Wharton

(knowledge.wharton.upenn.edu/category.cfm?catid=8)

A bi-weekly report on real estate insights and information.

Real Estate Research at the Haas Business School

(groups.haas.berkeley.edu/realestate/Research/researchinfo.asp)

Academic and market research provided by a top-ranked real estate graduate program.

Urban Land Institute

(www.uli.org)

A community of practice that has among its 25,000 members professors, urban planners, developers, and policy makers. The institute is dedicated to providing leadership in responsible land use in the urban environment.

WETFEET'S INSIDER GUIDE SERIES

Job Search Guides

Getting Your Ideal Internship

Job Hunting A to Z: Landing the Job You Want

Killer Consulting Resumes!

Killer Cover Letters & Resumes!

Killer Investment Banking Resumes!

Negotiating Your Salary & Perks

Networking Works!

Interview Guides

Ace Your Case: Consulting Interviews

Ace Your Case II: 15 More Consulting Cases

Ace Your Case III: Practice Makes Perfect

Ace Your Case IV: The Latest & Greatest

Ace Your Case V: Return to the Case Interview

Ace Your Interview!

Beat the Street: Investment Banking Interviews

Beat the Street II: I-Banking Interview Practice Guide

Career & Industry Guides

Careers in Accounting

Careers in Advertising & Public Relations

Careers in Asset Management & Retail Brokerage

Careers in Biotech & Pharmaceuticals

Careers in Brand Management

Careers in Consumer Products

Careers in Entertainment & Sports

Careers in Human Resources

Careers in Information Technology

Careers in Investment Banking

Careers in Management Consulting

Careers in Marketing & Market Research

Careers in Nonprofits & Government Agencies

Careers in Real Estate

Careers in Retail

Careers in Supply Chain Management

Careers in Venture Capital

Industries & Careers for MBAs

Industries & Careers for Undergrads

Specialized Consulting Careers: Health Care, Human Resources, and Information Technology

Company Guides

25 Top Consulting Firms

25 Top Financial Services Firms

Accenture

Bain & Company

Booz Allen Hamilton

Boston Consulting Group

Credit Suisse First Boston

Deloitte Consulting

The Goldman Sachs Group

J.P. Morgan Chase & Co.

Lehman Brothers

McKinsey & Company

Merrill Lynch & Co.

Morgan Stanley

UBS

WetFeet in the City Guides

Job Hunting in New York City

Job Hunting in San Francisco